W9-AUY-223

THE
OTHER
HEADING

JACQUES DERRIDA

THE OTHER HEADING

———╂———

REFLECTIONS ON TODAY'S EUROPE

TRANSLATED BY PASCALE-ANNE BRAULT
AND MICHAEL B. NAAS

INTRODUCTION BY MICHAEL B. NAAS

INDIANA UNIVERSITY PRESS

BLOOMINGTON & INDIANAPOLIS

©1992 by Indiana University Press

Originally published in French as *L'autre cap*,
©1991 by Les Editions de Minuit.

Manufactured in the United States of America

**Library of Congress
Cataloging-in-Publication Data**

Derrida, Jacques.
    [Autre cap. English]
    The other heading : reflections on today's
Europe / Jacques Derrida : translated by
Pascale-Anne Brault and Michael B. Naas ;
introduction by Michael B. Naas.
        p. cm. — (Studies in Continental
    thought)
    Translation of: L'autre cap.
    Includes bibliographical references.
    Contents: Today — The other heading —
Call it a day for democracy.
    ISBN 0-253-31693-6 (alk. paper)
    1. Europe—Civilization—1945– 2.
Discourse analysis. 3. Valéry, Paul, 1871–
1945—Political and social views. 4. Press and
politics—France. 5. Press and politics—
Europe. 6. Public opinion—France. 7. Public
opinion—Europe. I. Derrida, Jacques.
Démocratie ajournée. English. 1992. II. Title.
III. Series.
D1055.D4813   1992
940.55—dc20   91-47585

     1 2 3 4 5 96 95 94 93 92

CONTENTS

INTRODUCTION:
FOR EXAMPLE,
Michael B. Naas

No one today will set out to read Jacques Derrida's *The Other Heading* without some already determined orientation or direction, without a certain bearing if not an already charted course, without knowing, for example, where they have been, where they are headed, and what they can expect from the other shore. Even those who will have come across these pages by accident, shipwrecked here by chance or unknown winds, who will have sailed under no ideological flag, will already read with certain assumptions or expectations, certain fears or hopes, with a certain understanding, at the very least, of what it means to think, read, and write "about" politics in general and "about" Europe in particular.

This has no doubt always been the case, but it is especially true today. Because the po-

lemic surrounding the work of Jacques Derrida has spread beyond academic circles to become a regular issue in the popular media, one can almost speak today of a certain "public opinion" surrounding Derrida, his work, and all that has come to be associated and confused with his name, for example, deconstruc*tionism*, multiculturalism, political correctness, and the list keeps growing. This does not mean, of course, that there is uniform agreement about what Derrida's work is, stands for, or promises—far from it—but it does mean that insofar as it has been framed by public opinion it is called upon to present itself in a certain way. Subject to public opinion—subject, therefore, to what is never present as such in any particular institution or media form, subject to what nonetheless appears as natural as the light of day, Derrida's work is called upon today to stand up for evaluation and judgment, to stand out so that all of us together and each of us individually can take a stand towards it, say yes or no to it, and thus identify what can be expected not only today but any day from the other shore.

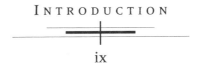
(For example, *just yesterday* [October 29, 1991] in an article in the *Chicago Tribune,* we read: ". . . deconstructionism, a French disease, was introduced to America at Yale. But it has spread, as French diseases will. . . . " I cite this example more for its status as an example, for its mere appearance in yesterday's hometown press, than for anything it might claim. For while its claims may be either mean-spiritedly misconceived or straightforwardly trite, the truth of the matter is that its example has spread, as public opinion will, to the point where one cannot but cite it.)

Yet even if the polemic is everywhere today, even if it is the very condition of reading and writing about philosophy or politics, this does not mean that everything is polemical—beginning with "today." While we may indeed have certain suspicions or hopes, while we perhaps must always set out in a particular direction with a compass and map in hand, it is not certain that we must always do so in order only to confirm, conquer, and condemn, in order only to rest assured that the other shore offers or promises us noth-

ing. For our reading would retain the *chance* of escaping mere repetition—and I am here repeating the opening of *The Other Heading*—the chance of not simply assuming public opinion in order then to take a position within it, insofar as it would analyze the conditions and contexts of public opinion, its forms of representation and repetition, of visibility, mediation, transmission, and translation. As Derrida said in an interview back in 1971:

> . . . I persist in believing that there is no theoretical or political benefit to be derived from precipitating contacts or articulations, as long as their conditions have not been rigorously elucidated. Eventually such precipitation will have the effect only of dogmatism, confusion, or opportunism.[1]

It seems that Derrida still persists in believing this, for *The Other Heading* is not so much an analysis of "Today's Europe"—if ever there were such a thing—as of the conditions and contexts for the debate "about" it; it is not so much an analysis of particular discourses

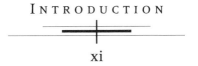
about Europe as of discourses that assume a certain relationship to the particular and the example; and it is not so much an analysis of particular public opinions as of the forms and means by which opinion becomes visible and effective.

For example, in newspapers. Derrida reminds us in "TODAY," his short preface to *The Other Heading,* that this little booklet or pamphlet is comprised of two articles, "The Other Heading: Memories, Responses, and Responsibilities" (1990), and "Call It a Day for Democracy" (1989), both of which were originally published in an abbreviated form in newspapers, that is, published on particular todays and brought to public attention in a "daily." This is important not only because the explicit theme of both articles is the media, but because the media never simply present or represent a theme without impressing themselves upon it in some way. Hence the style of *The Other Heading* will seem both more accessible, more immediately "applicable" to present-day political concerns, and

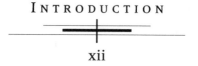
more elliptical, since accessibility is not won at the expense of Derrida's usual rigor and complexity. While these articles are surely not like those typically found in the editorial or political commentary pages of newspapers, they do share certain structural or rhetorical norms with them. Like any journalist, for example, Derrida had to agree that the final editorial authority would rest with the newspaper; like any other journalist, he had to assume a fairly broad and somewhat ill-defined context—even a public opinion—in which the article would be read; and in order to have the article both accepted and read, he had to address some "current event"—something of immediate social or political interest.

For example, the unification of Europe in 1992 or the bicentennial celebration of the French Revolution in 1989. But then the question is sure to be raised, "Why today? Why is Derrida beginning to write only today about politics? Does he simply wish to be back in the avant-garde, once again on the cutting edge, with a discourse about political

responsibility and a unified Europe?" This question is sure to be polemical, sure to be inflected with a tone of provocation or indictment, of critique or cynicism. It will never, in any case, be raised naively but always with too much certainty, too much faith in the terms of the question and the issues of the debate.

And so some will quickly respond that Derrida has always written about politics, that he has always had a political agenda, and that this is what makes him so dangerous, so "nihilistic" or "anti-humanistic." Others will respond just as quickly that he has *never* had a properly political agenda, and that *this* is what makes him so dangerous, so "nihilistic" or "anti-humanistic." Still others, speaking up from the other side, speaking out in defense or justification, perhaps even in celebration, will herald *The Other Heading* as a key to understanding a newly emerging Derridean politics. "Finally," they will say, "Derrida has provided us with a pragrammatological application of deconstructive theory to current political is-

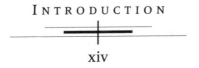
sues, a way to renew and radicalize the Enlightenment project, to fulfill the promise of a radical humanism.''

But whether one speaks for the prosecution or the defense, whether one sees in this work the same old heading, be it impotent or threatening, or a new direction, be it a radical departure from the past or the cautious unfolding of it, one will at a certain point have to *present* one's case. And if the argument is to be more than mere accusation or intuition, more than personal feeling or sentiment, one will have to provide a few *examples.*

For example, right here, in order to introduce or present *The Other Heading,* in order to portray it in any light, it would be necessary to give some examples of Derrida's argument and orientation in this and other works. For the task of an introduction is typically to situate the present work within the more general context of the author's life or intellectual itinerary, to demonstrate by means of a series of examples that the author has either

changed headings or kept to the same one. If, for example, one were to prove that Derrida has *always* been "political," that the political dimension of his thought has, in spite of all the differences between earlier and later texts, remained essentially the same, one would be expected to make a case by stringing together a series of texts and "todays" (for example, "The Ends of Man" (1968), "Racism's Last Word" (1983), "No Apocalypse, Not Now" (1984), "The Laws of Reflection: Nelson Mandela, in Admiration" (1986), etc.).[2] Such a procedure would be not only helpful but necessary, and I myself will not and could not avoid following it. But rather than simply citing *The Other Heading* as the most recent example of a coherent and consistent Derridean politics, I would rather let *The Other Heading* raise the question of politics from within a coherent and consistent critique of the logic of the example. For it just may be that, for Derrida, the logic of the example is always prior to, or at least complicitous with, the very notion of politics, in which case *The Other Heading* would be not

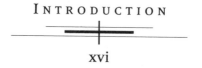
only an example of a Derridean discourse about politics but, insofar as it questions the logic of the example in political discourse, an exemplary place for thinking about the very meaning and possibility of a Derridean politics.

Derrida in fact begins *The Other Heading* by linking the question of European identity to the question of Europe as an example. Having just articulated a general law or axiom for all identity and self-identification, Derrida asks: "Will the Europe of yesterday, of tomorrow, and of today have been merely an example of this law? One example among others? Or will it have been the exemplary possibility of this law?"

Starting, then, not with an example of politics in the Derridean corpus—as if the example had nothing to do with the politics—but with the question of the example in *The Other Heading,* one might then cite a few examples from other works that would help us to understand this logic of the example. For instance, the following from Derrida's introduction to Husserl's *The Origin of Geometry:*[3]

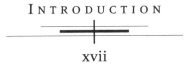
The ambiguity of an *example* that is at once an undistinguished *sample* and a teleological *model* is still found here. In the first sense, in fact, we could say with Husserl that every community is in history, that historicity is the essential horizon of humanity, insofar as there is no humanity without sociality and culture. From this perspective, any society at all, European, archaic, or some other, can serve as an example in an eidetic recognition. But on the other hand, Europe has the privilege of being the *good example,* for it incarnates in its purity the Telos of all historicity: universality, omnitemporality, infinite traditionality, and so forth; by investigating the sense of the pure and infinite possibility of historicity, Europe has awakened history to its own proper end. Therefore, in this second sense, pure historicity is reserved for the European *eidos.* The empirical types of non-European societies, then, are only *more or less* historical; at the lower limit, they *tend toward* nonhistoricity.

Is it a coincidence that what would seem to be a properly political analysis gets devel-

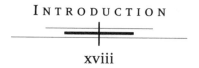
oped out of an analysis of the example? Is it possible that the question of the example is not simply one political question among many, that the question of politics is not merely one example of the question of the example, but that the question of the example essentially "is" the question of politics? For even if one attempted to read this analysis of Europe as an early application of deconstructive theory to a properly political concern, would not this very notion of application have difficulty extricating itself from the very same logic of the example? And inversely, if one attempted to read this analysis as merely an exemplary elaboration of deconstructive theory, would not such a notion of elaboration have difficulty escaping this very same politics of the example?

The Other Heading would seem to be consistent, then, with Derrida's constant coupling of politics and the example, with his persistent questioning of the relationship between nationalism and philosophical nationality, between national or supranational identity and the logic of identity itself. Even

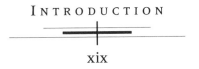
in Derrida's most "theoretical" works, and already from the very beginning, it seems that the identity of politics has always been complicitous with a certain politics of identity—with a politics of the mere particular and the putative example. And Europe has never been merely one example among many of this complicity:

In order to understand Europe it is necessary to begin with an idea, with a pure and *a priori* signification. This idea of Europe is the idea that is born in Europe; it is the idea of philosophy that is, in its absolute originality, as Husserl tells us, a European idea. In fact, Europe is not the cradle of philosophy, it is itself born as spiritual signification, from the idea of philosophy. . . . Husserl would not deny that in its empirical facticity Europe has no privileged relation with the idea of philosophy. And yet, as a spiritual place of birth, as the mysterious and immaterial residence of philosophy, Europe resists variation. A European *eidos* is here converging with the idea of philosophy. . . . At a certain moment, the pure idea of philosophy has

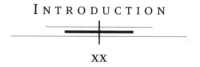
come to converge with the destiny and existence of a people or a group of people.

In a certain sense, this last example would seem to be the most conclusive, for it comes from Derrida's master's thesis of 1953–54, *The Problem of Genesis in the Philosophy of Husserl*.[4] Beginning here, one could in a quite traditional way multiply the examples of such analyses in the Derridean corpus to show that Derrida has been, for close to forty years now, one of the most insistent and self-consistent political thinkers of our time. Yet what exactly would be consistent about these various examples apart from the explicit interest in, the mere mentioning or mere use of, the example of politics or the politics of the example? How could we understand the consistency of a Derridean politics without merely assuming and thus recapitulating the logic of the example that is being criticized from *The Problem of Genesis in the Philosophy of Husserl* right up through *The Other Heading*?

Such questions concerning Derrida's own self-consistency may seem to be preliminary

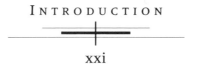
or even unrelated to the question of politics as such. Yet what if these questions were inseparable from all those concerning the relationship between politics and the discourse "about" politics, the relationship between political practice and theory, between the identity of politics, of politics as such, and the politics of identity? If such were the case, then one could never simply give examples of a Derridean politics without *at the same time* questioning one's own use of examples; one could never simply *present* a Derridean politics without at the same time implicating one's own presentation. (In the preface to *Of Grammatology*, for example, Derrida says that the "critical concepts" of the first part of that work are "put to the test" in the second part, "Nature, Culture, Writing," adding: "This is the moment, as it were, of the example, although strictly speaking, that notion is not acceptable within my argument."[5])

To say, then, as a sort of proposition or axiom, that it is nothing other than this critique of the example that has remained the same in Derrida's political thought is simply

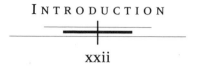
to open up in all its complexity the relationship between politics and the example, between a Derridean theory and a Derridean practice of politics and the example. It is to allow the possibility of beginning not with examples of Derrida's politics but with Derrida's critique of the political example, and thus not simply with Husserl's politics of Europe, but with his representation of Europe *as* an example, that is, with a Europe that is not simply one example among others—as it would feign to be—but the essentially "good example," the only possible one in fact—a particular, historical, and thus always political example. Such a reversal in the traditional order of politics and the example would allow the possibility of introducing *The Other Heading* not as an example of a Derridean politics but as an exemplary reading of the politics of the example; it would allow the possibility of beginning not with a politics of which we would then give examples, but with examples out of which we might *invent* a politics.

A politics of *The Other Heading*, for exam-

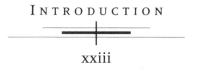
ple. Indeed the example is either mentioned or used (if we can still use this distinction) no less than forty times in this short book, mentioned—often under the name of "exemplarity"—or used, as in the phrase "for example," in order to show, if I might summarize, that in the West a certain political thinking of spirit and capital has always depended upon or entailed a mere mentioning and mere use of examples. By following the different situations and contexts of these examples in *The Other Heading,* by focusing on them *as* examples and not simply as examples of some general rule or concept, we might begin to see that the question of politics is, for Derrida, always a question of situation and context. And we might begin to understand the necessity of Derrida's "own" examples in *The Other Heading,* the necessity of all those elements that might appear merely occasional or contingent, merely personal or idiosyncratic.

For example, Valéry. A good part of "The Other Heading: Memories, Responses, and

Responsibilities" is devoted to a reading of
Paul Valéry's historical and political works—
works for which he is generally less well
known. And so the question is sure to be
raised, why Valéry's political works, and why
today, why read Valéry today unless to find
in him a model, example, or paradigm for
helping us to rethink European identity and
European unification in 1992? (Derrida
writes in "Qual Quelle: Valéry's Sources," a
lecture given in 1971 for the centennial of
Valéry's birth: "Valéry one hundred years
later, Valéry for us, Valéry now, Valéry today,
Valéry alive, Valéry dead—always the same
code."[6]) Once again, the answer, the response, lies in the context, since it always has
more than just a bearing on the heading.
Derrida first presented "The Other Heading:
Memories, Responses, and Responsibilities"
in May 1990 during a colloquium on European cultural identity in Turin—"a Latin
place of the northern Mediterranean." Now
it just so happens that Valéry was not only a
European intellectual but, as Derrida says, a
"Mediterranean spirit." Born today, or rather

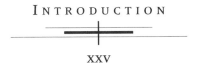
on *this* day (October 30) in 1871, to an Italian mother and a Corsican father, Paul Valéry saw in the European spirit an exemplary value for humankind and in the Mediterranean an exemplary value for Europe. For Valéry,

> [t]he best example, the only one in truth, the most irreplaceable, is that of the Mediterranean basin: the "example" that it "offered" is in fact unique, exemplary and incomparable. It is therefore not an example among others, and this is why *logos* and history are no longer separated, since this example will have been "the most striking and conclusive."

For Valéry, then, the Mediterranean in particular and Europe more generally have never been mere examples. To speak at a colloquium in Turin as if one were in Paris, for example, or London, or New York, or Peking, would already be to assume a certain logic of the example, a certain relationship between a particular place and the general notion of place—a particularly problematic assump-

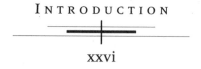
tion at a colloquium on "European cultural
identity." To have feigned to efface all these
marks of particularity, of context and situation, would have been to draw attention
away from the problematic nature of examples in political discourse, away from political discourse as an example, in order to
provide an exemplary, and thus universalist,
discourse about politics. It would have been
to inscribe a particular place and discourse *in
the name* of the universal. For the "value of
universality" is always, says Derrida

> linked to the value of *exemplarity* that in-
> scribes the universal in the proper body of a
> singularity, of an idiom or a culture, whether
> this singularity be individual, social, na-
> tional, state, federal, confederal, or not.

What makes Valéry exemplary is not that he
simply privileges Europe or the Mediterranean, but that he tries, not unlike Husserl, to
articulate a logic whereby the example or ex-
emplar would become a universal heading
for all the nations or peoples of the world.
Such a logic would thus not militate against,

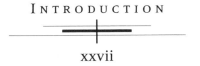
but might even promote, the unification of individual nations or peoples in the name of international law and universal values.

For example, in a League of Nations. Derrida begins *The Other Heading* by claiming that "something unique is afoot in Europe," something that "refus[es] itself to anticipation as much as to analogy," that "seems to be without precedent." And yet he also speaks of an imminence in Valéry "whose repetition we seem to be living," an imminence "that so much *resembles* our own, to the point where we wrongly and too precipitately borrow from it so many discursive schema." How are we to understand this apparent contradiction? How are we to understand resemblance when what is at stake is a certain logic of resemblance, of analogy and example—since it would seem that particular events become examples or analogies only insofar as they resemble each other in some way? In identifying certain similarities between two times or two thinkers, be they of this century or the last, be they German or

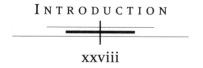
French, Derrida can therefore neither simply reject nor assume this notion of resemblance, since it is precisely the possibility of giving various examples of a general movement—such as a movement of "spirit"—that is being called into question:

> I note only that from Hegel to Valéry, from Husserl to Heidegger, in spite of all the differences that distinguish these great examples from each other—I tried to mark them elsewhere, in *Of Spirit* for example—this *traditional* discourse is *already* a discourse of the *modern* Western world. . . . This old discourse about Europe, a discourse at once exemplary and exemplarist, is already a *traditional discourse of modernity.*

Derrida cites his own *Of Spirit* as an example of this rethinking the example. Hegel, Valéry, Husserl, and Heidegger are "great examples," it seems, not because they all define Europe in terms of spirit, but because they all present Europe and spirit in terms of the logic of the example. These discourses thus resemble each other only insofar as they un-

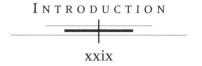
derstand resemblance—and thereby identify and recognize Europe—in a similar way.

> In its physical geography, and in what has often been called, by Husserl for example, its *spiritual geography,* Europe has always recognized itself as a cape or headland. . . .
>
> There was, for example, the form of the Hegelian moment wherein European discourse coincided with spirit's return to itself in Absolute Knowledge. . . .

Derrida's "for example" both works within the logic of the example and displaces it. For if Derrida were to present Husserl or Hegel as a mere example of a general movement that runs from Hegel to Valéry, he would in effect be treating Husserl as Husserl treated Europe, or treating Hegel as Hegel treated European discourse—that is, not only as one example among others for thinking this movement but as *the* exemplary place for it to be thought. For while Europe would *present itself* as just one example among many, it would, insofar as it articulates this very logic of the example, be *the* example of what remains

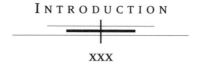
completely outside the discourse as its trans-
parent and unquestioned condition.

> Spirit is one of the categories of the analogy
> *and* the incomparable condition, the tran-
> scendental, the transcategorial of the whole
> economy. It is an example and an exemplary
> example, the example *par excellence.* There is
> no other.

Spirit would thus be its own condition; it
would make of itself the example *par excellence* and would thus orient all other examples toward it. (Spirit would thus function, in
a sense, like God. In "How to Avoid Speaking: Denials," Derrida says and emphasizes:
"In every prayer there must be an address to
the other as other; *for example*—I will say, at
the risk of shocking—*God.*"[7]) It is this orientation, this complicity between the example
and the universal, that Derrida sees as "similar" in the great philosophical discourses
about spirit from Hegel to Valéry.

> Refraining from giving any examples, let us
> emphasize for the moment a generality: in
> this struggle for control over culture, in this

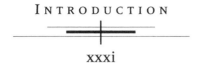
strategy that tries to organize cultural iden-
tity around a capital that is all the more
powerful for being mobile, that is, European
in a hyper- or supra-national sense, national
hegemony is not claimed—today no more
than ever—in the name of an empirical
superiority, that is to say, a simple particularity.

By working both within this logic and at
its limits, by not claiming to present it as
such, by not assuming either that one can
give mere examples of this logic or that one
can completely avoid it, Derrida allows us to
begin to think what is and has always been
unprecedented "in" this logic, what has organized this relationship between spirit and
itself, between the transcendental that would
seem to be outside the discourse and the examples within it. For if what links Hegel to
Valéry cannot be completely thought within
this logic of the example, then we are perhaps called upon to think a relation of *exemplarity* that would never become present as
such, that would never be thematizable, and
yet, since it would not exist somewhere prior

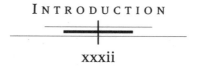
to any manifestation—as spirit might have
feigned to do—would always only appear as
an example of itself, an example that would
at once forbid and necessitate comparison
and resemblance. Such an exemplarity could
never function as a neutral or transparent
model or *telos* for discourse or thought. It
would necessitate thinking a resemblance
not between two present things but between
two thinkings of resemblance, a resemblance
between two examples that would illustrate
not some general rule or movement but only
their own exemplarity.

> Each time, the exemplarity of the example is
> unique. That is why it can be put into a se-
> ries and formalized into a law. Among all
> the possible examples, I will cite, yet again,
> only Valéry's, since I find it just as typical or
> archetypical as any other.

Such a rethinking of the example can
only be carried out "within" those discourses
where the logic of the example is at stake.
But this is hardly a limitation, for this logic is
at work everywhere today, and it is perhaps

not a coincidence that it is at work in what are generally called "political" discourses, that is, in discourses about national and supranational sovereignty and identity. Like Husserl's example of Europe, like Heidegger's example of Germany and the German language, Valéry's example of the Mediterranean, of Europe, of France, and even of Paris ("Valéry the Mediterranean, Valéry the European, wanted to be, in just as exemplary a way, the thinker of Paris"), turns out to have a privileged relationship to the very essence of humanity:

> The "exemplarist" logic that we are here trying to recognize had in fact driven Valéry . . . to present this capital . . . as the capital of capitals. . . . [B]y being distinguished in this way, the *exemplary* capital, our capital, is no longer simply the capital of a country, but the "head of Europe," and thus of the world, the capital of human society in general, or even better, of "human sociability."

Since the time of Fichte, numerous examples might attest to this. In the logic of

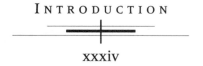
this "capitalistic" and cosmopolitical discourse, what is proper to a particular nation or idiom would be to be a heading for Europe; and what is proper to Europe would be, analogically, to advance itself as a heading for the universal essence of humanity.

For example—it bears repeating—as a heading for and as a League of Nations. In addition to having written many essays on Europe and European identity (in *Regards sur le monde actuel* and *Essais quasi politiques*), Valéry was a leading member of the Committee on Arts and Letters, which was established in 1931 by the League of Nations as a sort of permanent colloquium on "European cultural identity." And so just as the logic of the example both forbids and necessitates comparison between different philosophical discourses, so the task of thinking today, of thinking the today as the unprecedented, seems to both prohibit and demand a comparison between two times: between the years following World War I when a League of Nations was established and the years fol-

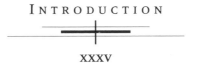
lowing the end of the Cold War, as important events in Eastern Europe and the Soviet Union coincide with the prospects of a unified Europe.

Is this the *same* Europe, then, that is being unified for a second time? Are these two moments in the history of a Europe whose configuration might change but whose essence would remain the same? Or is it possible that the current situation demands changing this traditional definition of Europe? Might not the task of thinking "Today's Europe" demand not only a new definition for European identity but a new way of thinking identity itself? And what if this rethinking of European identity were not a search for the radically new—since this is often precisely what the Old Europe sought or claimed—but the return to *another* origin of Old Europe, an origin that could never become the object of any search or discovery?

Derrida asks in the beginning of *The Other Heading* whether the today of Europe will break with this exemplary logic or whether the Europe of today will simply present itself,

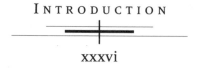
once again, as one example among others, and thus, as the exemplary possibility of the law to which it bears witness? In conjunction, therefore, with these more or less classic examples of philosophical discourse—Husserl, Heidegger, and most especially Valéry—Derrida cites a couple of recent texts from the French government that would claim for France an exemplary role in European politics and for today's Europe the opportunity for a joyous return to its origins and identity. But once again, what makes these claims significant is not simply what they say but the exemplarist logic they use in saying it. Thus when Derrida questions French President François Mitterrand's characterization of Europe's triumphant homecoming or reunion, he does so by implicitly relating the characterization itself to the logic of the example, referring to an *axiom* that would be "preliminary to the very possibility of giving a meaning to such assertions (for example, that of a 'reunion'). . . . " The notion of "reunion" is thus not merely an example of such assertions concerning European identity but an ex-

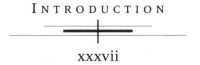
ample of the exemplarist logic by which
Europe would identify itself in terms of an
identifiable origin and end:

> The idea of an advanced point of *exemplarity* is
> the *idea of the* European *idea,* its *eidos,* at once
> as *arché*—the idea of beginning but also of
> commanding (the *cap* as the head, the place of
> capitalizing memory and of decision . . .)—
> and as *telos.* . . .

This advanced point is, according to Derrida,
a sort of avant-garde of memory and culture,
and so when "for example, . . . a certain official document coming out of the Ministry of
Foreign Affairs" refers to France's responsibility and "avant-garde position," its aim, its
mission even, in the "conquest of spirit(s)," it
is once again an exemplarist logic that is being invoked, the logic by which "France assigns herself this *exemplary* task." And when
Derrida cites the claims of "all French majorities" to an avant-garde status, he argues that
such claims are being made today, as in the
time of Valéry, in the name of a universal
idea:

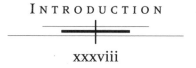
Without exception, they claim for France,
which is, of course, to say for Paris, for the
capital of all revolutions and for the Paris of
today, the role of the avant-garde, for example, in the idea of democratic culture, that is,
quite simply, of free culture itself, which is
founded on an idea of human rights, on an
idea of an international law.

One will have noticed that each time it
is a certain discourse about Europe that is being analyzed, a certain *presentation* or *self-
presentation* of Europe. It is thus not a question in *The Other Heading,* as some might
claim, of "reducing Europe to a text," or of
"deconstructing Europe," but of analyzing
those discourses "about" Europe that would
themselves claim or simply assume some relationship between discourse and Europe, between speaking about Europe and Europe
itself, and thus between language or spirit
and what is generally taken to be a geographical or spiritual entity outside or before all
language. In each case, Derrida analyzes discourses that thematize Europe's identity and
mission, Europe's place and distinction in the

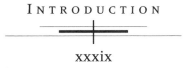
world. Each time, it is a question of a discourse that affirms Europe's role as an example of universality. Each time, then, it is a question of a discourse that presents Europe by means of a logic that was born and nurtured in Europe. And so each time, it is a question of an exemplary discourse for the logic of the example, an exemplary European discourse of universality.

This persistent critique of the logic of the example helps to explain why so many of Derrida's works are "occasional" pieces, and why the marks of the occasion are so often retained. For an occasion is always both an irreducibly singular event and, in as much as it takes place, that which necessitates comparison, contextualization, and analysis. Such attention to context and situation, to places and frameworks, can be found from the very beginning of *The Other Heading.*

For example, in the title, since a title is never simply an example of the work's content but a heading or orientation for all the other examples within it. This logic can also

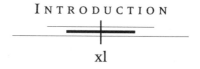
be found right in the beginning, where Derrida preserves in the written version of the text the idiosyncratic marks of its oral communication in Turin. Derrida begins by asking whether a colloquium on European cultural identity can avoid the risk of becoming "[j]ust another *cultural* event, for example, or a performance, or else an exercise in what one calls, with this very obscure word, 'culture.' " In other words, Derrida asks whether any colloquium on European cultural identity that did not take its own exemplarity into account would not end up recapitulating the logic of the example that sustains a traditional understanding of European identity, thereby neutralizing its political force. (As Derrida says in the beginning of his famous essay "The Ends of Man," first presented at a colloquium in October 1968 in New York: "Every philosophical colloquium necessarily has a political significance." And so in addition to speaking "about" politics, humanism, and democracy in this text, Derrida goes on to recall "the writing of this text, which I date quite precisely from the month of April 1968 . . . the weeks of the

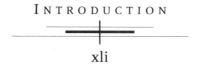

opening of the Vietnam peace talks and of
the assassination of Martin Luther King. A
bit later, when I was typing this text, the universities of Paris were invaded by the forces
of order. . . . ''[8]) Once again, it is necessary
both in fact and in principle to recall the
forms, structures, contexts, and values of
communication and language.

For example, the values of speaking or being read in another country or another language—in translation. (And so right here in
fact, in the middle of these examples, the
translators would like to recall and acknowledge their gratitude to their colleagues at
DePaul University, to Daryl Koehn, Bill Martin, Andrew Suozzo, and Lawrence Waxman
for their many fine suggestions, and especially to David Krell, for his encouragement,
hard work, good judgment, and guidance.
And of course, they would like to thank
Jacques Derrida, who must suffer to be ac-
knowledged yet again, and along with
others, for his exemplary kindness, patience,
and support.)

For the question of translation, the ques-

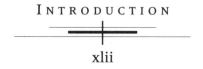
tion of when and whether to translate, of what linguistic capital will dominate in Europe in 1992, is never simply one question among many on the agenda—not in Derrida and not in any other serious discourse about Europe. Indeed the question of translation is often the very condition for talking about the agenda, for sitting down at the "same" table. And the same goes for communicating by telephone, radio, or television, since none of these is ever completely neutral or transparent. "For example,"—right here—since English is not today simply one language among others. (Just as French was not for Valéry, who, as Derrida says, linked the question of form in philosophy "to the national language and, in a singular and exemplary way, to the French language.") Derrida writes in the English version of "Two Words for Joyce":[9]

> . . . this hegemony remains indisputable, but its law only appears *as such* in the course of a *war* through which English tries to erase the other language or languages, to colonize

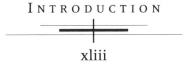
them, to domesticate them, to present them
for reading from only one angle. Which was
never so true. Today.

This *polemos* or war at the center of translation, at the very center of identity or being or
truth (*war*), must not be forgotten when Derrida speaks of the new European newspaper
Liber that links the todays of four European
centers—Turin, Madrid, Paris, and Frankfurt.
What does it mean, Derrida asks, for a newspaper published simultaneously in four different languages to be unified under a Latin
title or heading. Such a name would seem to
be in conformity with Derrida's notion of
paleonomy ("the "strategic" necessity that
requires the occasional maintenance of an *old
name* in order to launch a new concept"),[10]
but Derrida in effect asks whether the Latin
context is there in order to *liberate* us from it,
in order to point us toward an even more
radical liberation than the one that is sug-
gested by Latin roots, or whether it bids us
return to these roots in order to repeat and
celebrate them. Derrida asks, in effect,

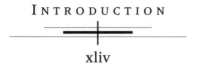
whether the imperative is to invoke the other from within *a* Latin idiom in order to liberate them from the hegemony of any particular idiom (*libère-toi*), to experiment with and thus reinvent an old language, or whether it is to call the other back to this idiom of liberation, to invoke a return to or rediscovery of an old language in all its lexical play and force.

For example, in the metaphor, if it is a metaphor, of navigation. Already in Plato's *Statesman* and *Republic,* for example, two discourses that have given the heading for all Western political discourse, the state is compared to a ship and the king to a captain. This metaphor reemerges in various forms in the West right up through Valéry, who sees in Europe a heading, *the* heading, for all intellectual and cultural discovery and speculation. Yet this very heading would seem to suggest that navigation could never be a *mere* metaphor, for one of the essential properties of this heading is the conversion of material goods into spiritual ones, that is, the metaphorization of literal goods and capital into the surplus

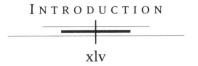
value, the capital value, of spirit. Once again, Derrida sees capital, like spirit, operating on two registers, one literal and the other metaphorical, or rather, one both literal and metaphorical and the other exceeding and responsible for both: "It is 'the very thing,' the 'capital point,' the thing itself that is divided between the two registers or two regimes of the analogy. For example:. . . . " Such, it would seem, is the very *telos* of capital, the overcoming of the merely material in a spiritual surplus, the capitalizing venture and return to a surplus value that will have already been there from the beginning—as the spirit or essence of Europe.

And so Derrida too sets out from a Europe that has always defined itself as the capital of culture, the headland of thought, in whose name and for whose benefit exploration of other lands, other peoples, and other ways of thinking has been carried out. He sets out from a Europe where the metaphor of navigation has always presented itself as a mere metaphor, where language and tropes have been ventured in the expectation that they

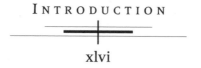
would return with an even greater value attached. If such Eurocentric biases are not to be repeated, Derrida warns, the question of Europe must be asked in a new way; it must be asked by recalling that "the other heading" is not a mere metaphor subject to capitalization, but the very condition of our metaphors, our language, and our thought.

Derrida argues not only that Europe *must* be responsible for the other, but that its own identity *is* in fact constituted by the other. Rejecting the easy or programmatic solutions of either complete unification ("The New World Order") or total dispersion, Derrida argues for the necessity of working with and from the Enlightenment values of liberal democracy while at the same time recalling that these values are never enough to ensure respect for the other. Derrida thus seeks a redefinition of European identity that includes respect for *both* universal values *and* difference—since one without the other will simply repeat without submitting to critique the politics of the example. (In his essay on Nelson Mandela, for example, Derrida shows

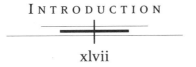
that Mandela is admirable not simply because of his particular form of resistance, nor simply because he is a good model of European, and thus universal, values, but because he is an exemplary and unique reflection of those values: "Why does [Mandela] seem exemplary—and admirable in what he thinks and says, in what he does or in what he suffers? Admirable in himself. . . . "[11]) If it is to be responsible for itself and for the other—for itself as other—then Europe must appeal both to its own heading and to the heading of the other, even, in the end, to the other of the heading, that is, to that which it cannot simply say yes or no to, take a position toward, affirm or deny, that which it cannot simply identify through examples but must think as exemplarity itself—the irreducible singularity of each example.

And so Derrida suggests that while we cannot and indeed must not avoid the language of responsibility and identity—for this would be to open ourselves up to the worst possible abuses (which, as Derrida reminds us, have always been perpetrated in the name of the ab-

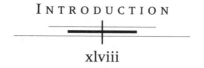
solutely new or different, in the name of an absolute break with the past)—neither can we simply afford to accept this language without submitting it to an interminable critique. If the Enlightenment has given us human rights, political liberties and responsibilities, it would surely be out of the question to want to do away with the Enlightenment project. But it may also be necessary not simply to affirm but to question the values it has given us, not to take them for granted but to take them as that which can never be completely taken or granted. The imperative remains, therefore, to return to these names and discourses precisely because they have given us our language— our language of responsibility, of giving, and of the example. The imperative remains, therefore, to question the exemplarity of this language and this heritage in order to encounter or experience what remains necessarily absent and unthought, necessarily without example, in them.

For example, to question the heritage of our language and thought in and through the

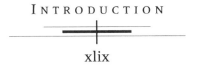
university. For while Derrida warns that a homogeneity of discourse might be imposed through a "new university space, and especially through a philosophical discourse" that would plead "for transparency," "for the univocity of democratic discussion, for communication in public space, for 'communicative action,'" a university might also provide the exemplary "space" or "forum" for *both* using *and* criticizing this logic of universality, for inventing an exemplarity that must remain without example or precedent, that would never be univocal, neutral, or transparent. Taking the necessary risk of an example, one might cite the Collège International de Philosophie as such a university space. Founded in 1984 by Derrida and others, the Collège is an example of a new pedagogical—and thus "political"—institution whose mission would be to present itself not as an exemplary place for education and communication but as an exemplary place for questioning the forms, structures, and institutions of education and communication—including the university. (In the description of his

1983–84 seminar entitled *Du droit à la philosophie,* a seminar given under the auspices of both the Collège and the Ecole normale supérieure, Derrida explains the necessity of questioning the foundation, legitimation, role, and structures of the philosophical institution in general, concluding: "The guiding thread for this preliminary attempt: the example of the Collège International de Philosophie. Is it a new 'philosophical institution'?"[12]) It was thus during a conference organized by the Collège in 1987 that Derrida first presented *Of Spirit,* a work about, among other things, Heidegger's relationship to the German state and university, to the language of philosophy and to the philosophy of language—and, of course, to spirit. Such a university would thus seem to be an exemplary place for teaching and learning about the politics of teaching and learning.

For example, teaching and learning philosophy—which will never be just one discipline among others. And so we might cite

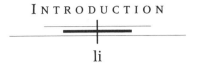
GREPH as another example of an organiza-
tion devoted to analyzing the exemplary status of philosophy. Founded in 1975 by
Derrida and others, Le Groupe de Recherches
sur l'Enseignement Philosophique is a group
of teachers and students devoted to asking
about the relationship between philosophy
and teaching, between the teaching of philosophy and the historical, political, social, and
economic conditions in which that teaching
takes place. GREPH is thus a "privileged"
place for asking about the exemplary status
of teaching and philosophy—a privileged
place for asking about the "nature" of the
example, and for acting upon these questions. In anticipation, therefore, of the formation of GREPH, Derrida said near the
beginning of his 1974–75 seminar: "There is
no neutral or natural place in teaching. Here,
for example, is not an indifferent place."[13]

Neither GREPH nor the Collège International de Philosophie would be, then, neutral
or natural places; neither, as Derrida has understood them, would be the transparent condition for talking about received ideas and

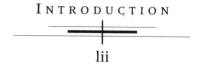
institutions. Rather, they would be exemplary places for asking about their own exemplarity, places for responding both to the particular and to that which exceeds it, both to the logic and exemplarity of the example. They would thus not be an exemplary response, not one response among many, certainly not *the* response, but a unique response to their own unprecedented situation, to what could never be a mere example.

Near the end of *The Other Heading,* Derrida gives some of his own *examples* of how we might best be responsible to and for the promise of what must remain without example. None of these examples claim to be mere examples, however; none present themselves as mere particulars that would essentially communicate with the universal. Indeed, each contains an antinomy that can be resolved only by ignoring either the example or the exemplarity of the example, either the necessary repeatability of a particular situation or its irreducible singularity. In each case, it is a question of a politics and ethics of the example:

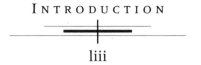
One could multiply the examples of this double duty. It would be necessary above all to discern the unprecedented forms that it is taking today in Europe. And not only to accept but to claim this putting to the test of the antinomy (in the forms, for example, of the double constraint, the undecidable, the performative contradiction, etc.). It would be necessary to recognize both the typical or recurring form and the inexhaustible singularization—without which there will never be any event, decision, responsibility, ethics, or politics.

For example, the inexhaustible singularization of today, of today's Europe—of a Europe that would resemble yesterday's or tomorrow's Europe only insofar as it, like them, would no longer resemble—and not even itself. Throughout the first part of *The Other Heading* Derrida speaks of a resemblance between the historical situation in which a League of Nations was formed and the situation we are now living with the unification of Europe; he even suggests a resemblance between his discourse, his position

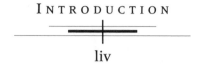
and status even, and Valéry's. And yet it is
clear, considering Derrida's sustained critique
of the logic of the example, that the League
of Nations and the Europe of 1992 cannot be
two mere examples of European unification,
just as Derrida and Valéry cannot be two
mere examples of French intellectuals. If par-
allels have to be drawn, if they *must* be
drawn, then it must also be kept in mind that
such lines and distinctions are never natural,
that their legitimacy is never simply given.
Hence Derrida ''identifies'' himself with
Valéry not in order to repeat or to do away
with the notion of identity but to reinvent it.
Rather than merely repeating Valéry's self-
identification in Europe, in the Mediterranean—in all those sources that reflect an
identity without opening it up onto the
other—rather than simply interrupting this
reflection so that there is no self-recognition
at all, Derrida demonstrates that self-
reflection and self-recognition only ever begin in a source or heading that is not ours.
(For example, in ''Qual Quelle: Valéry's
Sources,'' Derrida demonstrates that the

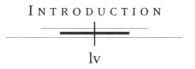
"logic of Valéry's aversions" corresponds not to a series of personal dislikes and fears but to a series of exemplary blind spots in Valéry's own self-reflection: "Here, for example, the names would be those of Nietzsche and Freud."[14] [Here, in *The Other Heading*, when Valéry identifies Europe as a "cape" or "appendix" to the Asian continent, the exemplary name might still be that of Nietzsche, who called "geographical Europe" the "little peninsula of Asia."[15]]) By recontextualizing a discourse that would have feigned to give up its particularity in the name of a universal, Derrida demonstrates the irreducible singularity of Valéry's discourse—and it is precisely with this irreducible singularity, with what can have no example, that Derrida identifies himself, his situation, and his time. Thus when Derrida repeats or "mimes" Valéry's own attempt to pass off a personal feeling for a general axiom, he not only draws attention to Valéry's strategy but, by citing or contextualizing it *as* he uses it, presents it as an example of what can no longer simply be presented, that is, as an example of

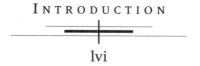
the exemplary relationship between the personal and the general, between one today and all todays, between himself and Valéry, between himself and all other Europeans:

> Out of this feeling of an old, anachronistic European . . . I will make the *first axiom* of this little talk. And I will say "we" in place of "I," another way of moving surreptitiously from the feeling to the axiom.

But what if this axiom did not simply assume the logic of the example but problematized it, if it claimed that every example were an example not of some general notion of identity but of an exemplarity that both constitutes and disrupts the identity of all examples? Then, it seems, the axiom would reintroduce not only the personal and the particular—the possibility of other headings—but the irreducible singularity or exemplarity that would allow for the "unification"—though never the subsumption—of these particulars—the other of the heading. It would thus require not simply abandoning the notion of exemplarity but

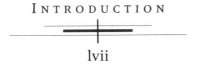
reinscribing it, allowing for a Europe that would not be "guided by the idea of a transcendental community, the subjectivity of a 'we' for which Europe would be at once the name and the exemplary figure," but a Europe that would "advanc[e] itself in an exemplary way toward what it is not . . . ," a Europe that would be exemplary in this very openness.

The other of the heading would require us to rethink not only our notion of identity and the example, but our notion of the identity of today as a mere example; it would require us to think the irreducible singularity of a day, another day, that would actually constitute our day. It would require us to think the necessity of not only a new revolution in Enlightenment values but a revolution in this notion of revolution and Enlightenment.

I began this introduction by talking about *The Other Heading*'s emphasis on the media, on public opinion, and on certain freedoms in and of the press. At the end of "Call It a Day for Democracy," Derrida seems to suggest that these values and freedoms, the heri-

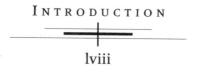
tage of—for example—the French and American Revolutions, conceal and call out for a revolution that can have no examples— a revolution in the forms of visibility and mediation that the media and public opinion assume, a revolution, therefore, in the very order of the day, and thus, in the very promise and politics of the example.

NOTES

1. Jacques Derrida, *Positions,* trans. Alan Bass (Chicago: University of Chicago Press, 1981), p. 62.

2. For an excellent bibliography of Derrida's work, see *A Derrida Reader,* ed. Peggy Kamuf (New York: Columbia University Press, 1991), pp. 601–12.

3. Jacques Derrida, *Edmund Husserl's "Origin of Geometry": An Introduction,* translated, with a preface, by John P. Leavey, Jr. (Stony Brook, N.Y.: Nicholas Hays, Ltd., 1978), p. 115.

4. Jacques Derrida, *Le problème de la genèse dans la philosophie de Husserl* (Paris: Presses Universitaires de France, 1990), pp. 250–51.

5. Jacques Derrida, *Of Grammatology,* trans. Gayatri Chakravorty Spivak (Baltimore: Johns Hopkins University Press, 1976), p. lxxxix.

6. In Jacques Derrida, *Margins of Philosophy,* trans.

Alan Bass (Chicago: University of Chicago Press, 1982), p. 278.

7. Jacques Derrida, "How to Avoid Speaking: Denials," in *Languages of the Unsayable*, trans. Ken Freiden, ed. Sanford Budick and Wolfgang Iser (New York: Columbia University Press, 1989), p. 41.

8. Jacques Derrida, "The Ends of Man," in *Margins of Philosophy*, trans. Alan Bass (Chicago: University of Chicago Press, 1982), pp. 111, 114.

9. Jacques Derrida, "Two Words for Joyce," in *Post-Structuralist Joyce: Essays from the French*, ed. Derek Attridge and Daniel Ferrer (Cambridge: Cambridge University Press, 1984), pp. 47–48.

10. *Positions*, p. 71.

11. Jacques Derrida, "The Laws of Reflection: Nelson Mandela, in Admiration," trans. Mary Ann Caws and Isabelle Lorenz, in *For Nelson Mandela*, ed. Jacques Derrida and Mustapha Tlili (New York: Seaver Books, 1987), p. 13.

12. Jacques Derrida, "Privilège: Titre justificatif et remarques introductives," in *Du droit à la philosophie* (Paris: Editions Galilée, 1990), p. 11.

13. Jacques Derrida, "Où commence et comment finit un corps enseignant," in *Du droit à la philosophie*, p. 114.

14. *Margins of Philosophy*, p. 275.

15. Friedrich Nietzsche, *Human, All Too Human*, trans. R. J. Hollingdale (Cambridge: Cambridge University Press, 1986), p. 365.

THE
OTHER
HEADING

TODAY

By kindly asking me to publish in book form—as an opuscule or "booklet"—what was first a newspaper article, Jérôme Lindon led me to reflect upon the alliance of an accident and a necessity. Until then I had not paid enough attention to the fact that an article, "The Other Heading" [*L'autre cap*], clearly preoccupied with questions of the newspaper and the book, questions of publication, of the press, and of media culture, had itself been published in a newspaper (*Liber, Revue européenne des livres,* October 1990, no. 5). To be sure, it is a singular newspaper, one that tries to be the exception to the rule, since it is, in an

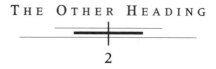
unusual way, inserted simultaneously into other European newspapers (*Frankfurter Allgemeine Zeitung, L'Indice, El Pais, Le Monde*) and thus at once into four different languages.

Now it just so happens, in an apparently fortuitous way, that another article, "Call It a Day for Democracy" [*La démocratie ajournée*], which in the end treats analogous problems—above all, problems concerning the press and publication, the relationship of newspapers, books, and the media to public opinion, to freedoms, human rights, democracy, and to Europe—had also been published the year before in *another* newspaper that was also the *same* one, that is, *Le Monde,* and again, *separately,* in the supplement of a special issue: the first issue of *Le Monde de la Révolution française* (January 1989), which appeared twelve times during the bicentennial year. But beyond this sharing of themes, and because of this *situation* (a newspaper *within* a newspaper but also a newspaper issued *separately*), I thought there was some sense in putting these two articles together as they were, side by side and under

the same light of day. For it is precisely the *day*, the question or reflection of the *day*, the resonance of the word *today*, that these daily articles still have most in common—at that date, on that day. Will the hypotheses and propositions thus ventured here turn out to be, for all that, dated today, in the midst of what is called the "Gulf" war, at a moment when the problems of law, public opinion, and media communication, among others, have come to have the urgency and gravity that we all know? This is for the reader to judge.

Today happens to be the first word of "Call It a Day for Democracy." Even if it is not the last word—especially not that—it corresponds perhaps in some way with what resonates strangely in the apostrophe of Paul Valéry that is cited at the beginning of "The Other Heading" and is then tossed out from time to time: "What are you going to do TODAY?"

January 29, 1991

THE
OTHER HEADING:
MEMORIES,
RESPONSES, AND
RESPONSIBILITIES

Acolloquium always tries to forget the risk it runs: the risk of being just another one of those events [*spectacles*] where, in good company, one strings together a few talks or speeches on some general subject. Just another *cultural* event, for example, or a performance, or else an exercise in what one calls, with this very obscure word, "culture." And an exercise

---

Before its publication in an abbreviated form in *Liber,* this paper was delivered in Turin on May 20, 1990, during a colloquium on "European Cultural Identity." The conference was presided over by Gianni Vattimo, with the participation of Maurice Aymard, Vladimir K. Bukovsky, Agnès Heller, José Saramago, Fernando Savater, and Vittorio Strada. The notes were, obviously, added after the fact.

around a question that will always be of current interest: Europe.

If this meeting had any chance of escaping repetition, it would be only insofar as some *imminence,* at once a chance and a danger, exerted pressure on us.

What imminence? Something unique is afoot in Europe, in what is still called Europe even if we no longer know very well *what* or *who* goes by this name. Indeed, to what concept, to what real individual, to what singular entity should this name be assigned today? Who will draw up its borders?

Refusing itself to anticipation as much as to analogy, what announces itself in this way seems to be without precedent. An anguished experience of imminence, crossed by two contradictory certainties: the very old subject of cultural identity in general (before the war one would have perhaps spoken of "spiritual" identity), the very old subject of European identity indeed has the venerable air of an old, exhausted theme. But perhaps this "subject" retains a virgin body. Would not its name mask something that does not yet have

a face? We ask ourselves in hope, in fear and trembling, what this face is going to resemble. Will it still resemble? Will it resemble the face of some *persona* whom we believe we know: Europe? And if its non-resemblance bears the traits of the future, will it escape monstrosity?

Hope, fear, and trembling are commensurate with the signs that are coming to us from everywhere in Europe, where, precisely in the name of identity, be it cultural or not, the worst violences, those that we recognize all too well without yet having thought them through, the crimes of xenophobia, racism, anti-Semitism, religious or nationalist fanaticism, are being unleashed, mixed up, mixed up with each other, but also, and there is nothing fortuitous in this, mixed in with the breath, with the respiration, with the very "spirit" of the promise.

To begin, I will confide in you a feeling. Already on the subject of headings [*caps*]—and of the shores on which I intend to remain. It is the somewhat weary feeling of an old European. More precisely, of someone who, not

quite European by birth, since I come from the southern coast of the Mediterranean, considers himself, and more and more so with age, to be a sort of over-acculturated, over-colonized European hybrid. (The Latin words *culture* and *colonialization* have a common root, there where it is precisely a question of what happens to roots.) In short, it is, perhaps, the feeling of someone who, as early as grade school in French Algeria, must have tried to capitalize, and capitalize upon, the old age of Europe, while at the same time keeping a little of the indifferent and impassive youth of the other shore. Keeping, in truth, all the marks of an ingenuity still incapable of this other old age from which French culture had, from very early on, separated him.

Out of this feeling of an old, anachronistic European, youthful and tired of his very age, I will make the *first axiom* of this little talk. And I will say "we" in place of "I," another way of moving surreptitiously from the feeling to the axiom.

We are younger than ever, we Europeans, since a certain Europe does not yet exist. Has

it ever existed? And yet we are like these young people who get up, at dawn, already old and tired. We are already exhausted. This *axiom of finitude* is a swarm or storm of questions. From what state of exhaustion must these young old-Europeans who we are set out again, re-embark [*re-partir*]? Must they re-begin? Or must they *depart* from Europe, separate themselves from an old Europe? Or else depart again, set out toward a Europe that does not yet exist? Or else re-embark in order to return to a Europe of origins that would then need to be restored, rediscovered, or reconstituted, during a great celebration of "reunion" [*retrouvailles*]?

"Reunion" is today an official word. It belongs to the code of French cultural politics in Europe. Ministerial speeches and documents make great use of it; they help explain a remark of François Mitterrand, the President of the Republic, who said (perhaps while also presiding over the European Community) that Europe "is returning in its history and its geography like one who is returning home" [*chez soi*]. What does this mean? Is it possible? Desirable? Is it really this that announces itself *today*?

I will not even try, not yet, to answer or respond to these questions. But I will venture a *second axiom.* I believe it to be preliminary to the very possibility of giving a meaning to such assertions (for example, that of a "reunion") and such questions. In spite of the inclination and conviction that should lead me to analyze genealogically the concepts of identity or culture—like the proper name of Europe—I must give this up, since the time and place do not lend themselves to it. I must nonetheless formulate in a somewhat dogmatic way, and this is my second axiom, a very dry necessity whose consequences could affect our entire problematic: *what is proper to a culture is to not be identical to itself.* Not to not have an identity, but not to be able to identify itself, to be able to say "me" or "we"; to be able to take the form of a subject only in the non-identity to itself or, if you prefer, only in the difference *with itself* [*avec soi*]. There is no culture or cultural identity without this difference *with it-*

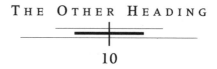
self. A strange and slightly violent syntax: "with itself" [*avec soi*] also means "at home (with itself)" [*chez soi*] (with, *avec,* is *"chez," apud hoc*). In this case, self-difference, difference to itself [*différence à soi*], that which differs and diverges from itself, of itself, would also be the *difference (from) with itself* [*différence (d') avec soi*], a difference at once internal and irreducible to the "at home (with itself)" [*chez soi*]. It would gather and divide just as irreducibly the center or hearth [*foyer*] of the "at home (with itself)." In truth, it would gather this center, relating it to itself, only to the extent that it would open it up to this divergence.

This can be said, inversely or reciprocally, of all identity or all identification: there is no self-relation, no relation to oneself, no identification with oneself, without culture, but a culture of oneself *as* a culture *of* the other, a culture of the double genitive and of the *difference to oneself.* The grammar of the double genitive also signals that a culture never has a single origin. Monogenealogy would al-

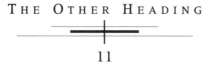
ways be a mystification in the history of culture.

Will the Europe of yesterday, of tomorrow, and of today have been merely an example of this law? One example among others? Or will it have been the exemplary possibility of this law? Is one more faithful to the heritage of a culture by cultivating the difference-to-oneself (*with oneself*) that constitutes identity or by confining oneself to an identity wherein this difference remains *gathered*? This question can have the most disquieting effects on all discourses and politics of cultural identity.

In his "Notes on the Greatness and Decline of Europe," Valéry seems to provoke a familiar interlocutor, one at once close and still unknown. In a sort of apostrophe, like the first pitch of a question that would no longer leave him in peace, Valéry tosses out to his interlocutor the word "today." "TODAY," the word is written in *capital* letters; today heightened like the challenge itself. The great challenge, the capital challenge, is

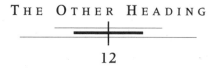
the day of *today,* the day of this day and age: "Well! What are you going to do? What are you going to do TODAY?"*

Why would the *day of today,* the day of this day and age, deserve capital letters? Because what we find difficult to do and think today, for Europe, for a Europe torn away from self-identification as repetition of itself, is precisely the unicity of the "today," a certain event, a singular advent of Europe, here and now. Is there a completely new "today" of Europe, a "today" whose novelty would not resemble—especially not—what was called by another well-known program, and one of the most sinister, a "New Europe"? We come across traps of this sort at every step, and they are not merely traps of language; they are part of the program. Is there then a completely new "today" of Europe beyond all the exhausted programs of *Eurocentrism* and *anti-*

---

*Paul Valéry, "Notes sur la grandeur et décadence de l'Europe," Vol. II of *Oeuvres Complètes* (Paris: Pléiade, 1960), p. 931 ["Notes on the Greatness and Decline of Europe," in *History and Politics,* trans. Denise Folliot and Jackson Mathews (New York: Bollingen, 1962), p. 228]. Quoted translations have been slightly modified.—Trans.

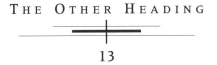
Eurocentrism, these exhausting yet unforgetta-
ble programs? (We cannot and must not forget them since they do not forget us.) Am I
taking advantage of the "we" when I begin
saying that, in knowing them now by heart,
and to the point of exhaustion—since these
unforgettable programs are exhausting and
exhausted—we *today* no longer want either
Eurocentrism or anti-Eurocentrism? Beyond
these all too well-known programs, for what
"cultural identity" must we be responsible?
And responsible before whom? Before what
memory? For what promise? And is "cultural
identity" a good word for "today"?

A title is always a heading [*cap*]. A chapter
heading, a headline, even a letterhead. By
proposing the title "The Other Heading" for
some brief, quasi-improvised reflections, I
was thinking at first, while on board a plane,
of the language of air or sea navigation. On
the sea or in the air, a vessel has a "heading": it "heads off," toward another continent, perhaps, toward a destination that is its
own but that it can also change. One says in
my language *"faire cap"* but also *"changer de*

cap''—to ''have a heading'' but also to ''change headings.'' The word *''cap''* (*caput, capitis*) refers, as you well know, to the head or the extremity of the extreme, the aim and the end, the ultimate, the last, the final moment or last legs, the *eschaton* in general. It here assigns to navigation the pole, the end, the *telos* of an oriented, calculated, deliberate, voluntary, ordered movement: ordered most often by the *man* in charge. Not by a woman, for in general, and especially in wartime, it is a *man* who decides on the heading, from the advanced point that he himself is, the prow, at the head of the ship or plane that he pilots. Eschatology and teleology—that is man. It is *he* who gives orders to the crew, he who holds the helm or sits at the controls; he is the headman, there at the head of the crew and the machine. And oftentimes, he is called the *captain.*

The expression ''The Other Heading'' can also suggest that another direction is in the offing, or that it is necessary to change destinations. To change direction can mean to change goals, to decide on another heading,

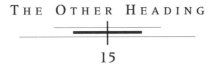

or else to change captains, or even—why not?—the age or sex of the captain. Indeed it can mean to recall that there is another heading, the heading being not only ours [*le nôtre*] but the other [*l'autre*], not only that which we identify, calculate, and decide upon, but the *heading of the other*, before which we must respond, and which we must *remember, of which* we must *remind ourselves,* the heading of the other being perhaps the first condition of an identity or identification that is not an egocentrism destructive of oneself and the other.

But beyond *our heading*, it is necessary to recall ourselves not only to the *other heading*, and especially to the *heading of the other*, but also perhaps to the *other of the heading*, that is to say, to a relation of identity with the other that no longer obeys the form, the sign, or the logic of the heading, nor even of the *anti-heading*—of beheading, of decapitation. The true title* of these reflections, even though a

---

*A *vrai titre,* a true title, may be opposed to a *faux titre,* a false or bastard title. Cf. John Leavey's introduction to Derrida's *The Archeology of the Frivolous* (Lincoln: University of Nebraska Press, 1980), pp. 14ff.—Trans.

title is a heading or headline, would orient us rather toward the other *of* the heading. By selection, I will deduce the form of all my propositions from a grammar and syntax of the heading, of the *cap,* from a difference in kind and gender [*genre*], that is, from *capital* and *capitale.** How can a ''European cultural identity'' respond, and in a responsible way—responsible for itself, for the other, and before the other—to the double question of *le capital,* of capital, and of *la capitale,* of the capital?

Europe today, in the *today* that Valéry writes in capital letters, is at a moment in its history (*if* it has one, and indeed is *one,* i.e., identifiable), in the history of its culture (if it can ever be identified as one, as the same, and can be responsible for itself, answer for itself, in a memory of itself) when the question of the heading seems unavoidable. Whatever the answer may be, the question

*Derrida plays throughout on the relationship between the feminine *la capitale,* the capital city of a country, and the masculine *le capital,* capital in the monetary sense.—Trans.

remains. I would even say that this is neces-
sary: it should remain, even beyond all an-
swers. No one today in fact thinks of
avoiding such a question, and this, not only
because of what has started, or rather has accelerated, these past few months in the east
or at the center of Europe. This question is
also very old, as old as the history of Europe,
but the experience of the *other heading* or of
the other *of* the heading presents itself in an
absolutely new way, not new "as always"
[*comme toujours*], but newly new. And what if
Europe were this: the opening onto a history
for which the changing of the heading, the
relation to the other heading or to the other
of the heading, is experienced as always possible? An opening and a non-exclusion for
which Europe would in some way be responsible? For which Europe *would be,* in a constitutive way, this very responsibility? As if the
very concept of responsibility were responsible, right up to its emancipation, for a European birth certificate?

Like every history, the history of a culture
no doubt presupposes an identifiable head-

ing, a *telos* toward which the movement, the memory, the promise, and the identity, even if it be as difference to itself, dreams of gathering itself: *taking the initiative, being out ahead, in anticipation* (*anticipatio, anticipare, antecapere*). But history also presupposes that the heading not be *given,* that it not be identifiable in advance and once and for all. The irruption of the new, the unicity of the other *today* should be awaited *as such* (but is the *as such,* the phenomenon, the being *as such* of the unique and of the other, ever possible?); it should be anticipated *as* the unforeseeable, the *unanticipatable,* the non-masterable, non-identifiable, in short, as that of which one does not yet have a memory. But our old memory tells us that it is *also* necessary to anticipate and to keep the heading [*garder le cap*], for under the banner—which can also become a slogan—of the unanticipatable or the absolutely new, we can fear seeing return the phantom of the worst, the one we have already identified. We know the "new" only too well, or in any case the old rhetoric, the demagogy, the psychagogy of the "new"—

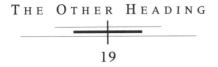
and sometimes of the "new order"—of the surprising, the virginal, and the unanticipatable. We must thus be suspicious of *both* repetitive memory *and* the completely other of the absolutely new; of *both* anamnestic capitalization *and* the amnesic exposure to what would no longer be identifiable at all.

A moment ago, I alluded to the tremor that is shaking what are called Central and Eastern Europe under the very problematic names *perestroika, democratization, reunification,* entry into the *market economy,* access to political and economic liberalisms. This earthquake, which by definition knows no borders, is no doubt the immediate cause of the subject chosen for this debate on "European cultural identity." I wanted to recall what has *always* identified Europe with a cape or headland [*cap*]. Always, since day one [*depuis toujours*], and this "day one" says something about all the days of today in the memory of Europe, in the memory of itself as the culture of Europe. In its physical geography, and in what has often been called, by Husserl for example, its *spiritual geography,*

Europe has always recognized itself as a cape or headland, *either* as the advanced extreme of a continent, to the west and south (the land's end, the advanced point of a Finistère,* Europe of the Atlantic or of the Greco-Latino-Iberian shores of the Mediterranean), the point of departure for discovery, invention, and colonization, *or* as the very center of this tongue in the form of a cape, the Europe of the middle, coiled up, indeed compressed along a Greco-Germanic axis, at the very center of the center of the cape.

That is in fact how Valéry *described and defined* Europe: as a cape, a headland; and, if this *description* had the form of a *definition,* it was because the concept corresponded to the border. It is the whole history of this geography. Valéry observes, looks at and *envisages* Europe; he sees in it a face [*visage*], a *persona,* and he thinks of it as a leader [*chef*], that is, as a head [*cap*]. This head also has eyes, it is

---

*Finistère is a region of Brittany on the westernmost coast of France, though Derrida is also drawing attention to the more general notion of a *finis terrae* or "land's end."— Trans.

turned to one side, and it scans the horizon, keeping watch in a determined direction:

> *Out of all these achievements, most, and the most astonishing and fruitful, have been the work of a tiny portion of humanity, living in a very small area compared to the whole of the habitable lands.*
>
> This privileged place was Europe; and the European man, the European spirit, was the author of these wonders.
>
> What, then, is Europe? It is a kind of cape of the old continent, a western appendix to Asia. It looks naturally toward the west. On the south it is bordered by a famous sea whose role, or I should say function, has been wonderfully effective in the development of that European spirit with which we are concerned.[1]

A cape, a little geographical promontory, an "appendix" to the body and to the "Asian continent," such *is* in Valéry's eyes the very essence of Europe, its *real being.* And in the at once provocative and classic paradox of this grammar, the first question of being and time *will have been* teleological, or rather counter-teleological: if such *is* its *essence,* will Europe

one day become what it is (not such a big deal after all, a little cape or appendix) or will it persist in what is not its essence but its *appearance,* that is, under the cap, the "brain"? And the true *telos,* the best, would here be on the side not of essence but of appearance. Valéry likes to say, in fact, and as if in passing, that this is the "capital" question.

> Now, the present day brings with it this capital question: Can Europe maintain its preeminence in all fields?
>
> Will Europe become *what it is in reality*— that is, a little promontory [*cap*] on the Asian continent?
>
> Or will it remain *what it seems*—that is, the elect portion of the terrestrial globe, the pearl of the sphere, the brain of a vast body?[2]

I interrupt for a moment my recapitulation of all these chapter headings [*caps*] or heads, in order to note that present here at this table are mostly *men* and citizens of Western Europe, writers or philosophers according to the classic model of the European intellec-

tual: a guardian held responsible for memory
and culture, a citizen entrusted with a sort of
spiritual mission of Europe. There are no English here—even though the Anglo-American
language is today the second universal language destined to overtake or dub all the idioms of the world; and this is one of the
essential problems of culture today, of European culture in particular, of which Anglo-
American both is and is not a language.
(When a French intellectual goes to Moscow—and I've had this experience so common to all of us—Anglo-American remains
the mediating language, as it is here at this
table for two of us, Agnès Heller and Vladimir
Bukovsky, who in fact come from neither
Hungary nor the U.S.S.R. but from major
Anglo-Saxon universities.) We are thus here
in a large majority male representatives of the
continental point or tip of the European
headland, in what is called the European
Community, which is predominantly Mediterranean. An accident or a necessity, these
traits are at once discriminant and significant.
They appear at least emblematic, and what I

hesitate to advance here under the title of "heading," of the *other* heading and of the other *of the heading*, would come to be inscribed, at least obliquely, under this sign.

Europe is not only a geographical headland or heading that has always given itself the representation or figure of a spiritual heading, at once as project, task, or infinite—that is to say universal—idea, as the memory of itself that gathers and accumulates itself, capitalizes upon itself, in and for itself. Europe has also confused its image, its face, its figure and its very place, its taking-place, with that of an advanced point, the point of a phallus if you will, and thus, once again, with a heading for world civilization or human culture in general. The idea of an advanced point of *exemplarity* is the *idea of the* European *idea*, its *eidos*, at once as *arché*—the idea of beginning but also of commanding (the *cap* as the head, the place of capitalizing memory and of decision, once again, the captain)—and as *telos*, the idea of the end, of a limit that accomplishes, or that puts an end to the whole point of the achievement, right

there at the point of completion. The advanced point is at once beginning and end, it is divided as beginning and end; it is the place from which or in view of which everything takes place. (When Heidegger defines place, *Ort,* he recalls that in its High or Old German idiom, *Ort* refers to the point of a spear, there where all the forces are joined and gathered in the end; and when he says that questioning is the piety of thinking, he recalls that *fromm, Frömmigkeit,* comes from *promos:* what comes first, *leads,* or directs the front line [*l'avant-garde*] in a battle.³)

It is always in the figure of the *Western* heading and of the *final* headland or point that Europe determines and cultivates itself; it is in this figure that Europe identifies itself, identifies with itself, and thus identifies its own cultural identity, in the being-for-itself of what is most proper to it, in its own difference as difference with itself, difference to itself that remains with itself, close to itself. Yes, difference *with itself, with the self* that is maintained and gathered in its own difference, in its difference *from-with* [*d'avec*] the

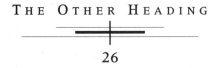
others, if one can say this, as difference to itself, different *from itself* for itself, in the temptation, risk, or chance of keeping at home (with itself) [*chez soi*] the turbulence of the *with,* of calming it down in order to make it into a simple, interior border—well guarded by the vigilant sentinels of being.

I should myself interrupt these recollections and change headings. We all know this program of Europe's self-reflection or self-presentation. We are old, I say it again. Old Europe seems to have exhausted all the possibilities of discourse and counter-discourse about its own identification. Dialectic in all its essential forms, including those that comprehend and entail anti-dialectic, has always been in the service of this autobiography of Europe, even when it took on the appearance of a confession. For avowal, guilt, and self-accusation no more escape this old program than does the celebration of self. Perhaps identification in general, the formation and affirmation of an identity, self-presentation, the self-presence of identity (whether it be national or not, cultural or not—even

though identification is itself always cultural
and never natural, for it is nature's way out
of itself in itself, nature's difference *with itself*), always has a capital form, the figurehead [*figure de proue*] of the advanced point,
and of capitalizing reserve.* It is thus not
only for lack of time that I will spare you the
development of a counter-program opposed
to this archeo-teleological program of all European discourse about Europe. I note only
that from Hegel to Valéry, from Husserl to
Heidegger, in spite of all the differences that
distinguish these great examples from each
other—I tried to mark them elsewhere, in *Of
Spirit* for example—this *traditional* discourse
is *already* a discourse of the *modern* Western
world. It dates, it is dated. It is the most current, nothing is more current, but already it
dates back. And this currentness reveals a fa-
miliarly disquieting wrinkle, discrete but
merciless, the very stigmata of an anachrony

---

*Prou in Old French means much or many, even too
much or too many. It is related to prowess and profit.—
Trans.

that marks the day of all our days, of all our gestures, discourses, and affects, both public and private. It dates from a moment when Europe sees itself *on the horizon,* that is to say, from its end (the *horizon,* in Greek, is the limit), from the imminence of its end. This old discourse about Europe, a discourse at once exemplary and exemplarist, is already a *traditional discourse of modernity.* It is also the discourse of anamnesis because of this refined taste for finality,* for the end, if not for death.

Now, we must ourselves be responsible for this discourse of the modern tradition. We bear the responsibility for this heritage, right along with the capitalizing memory that we have of it. We did not choose this responsibility; it imposes itself upon us, and in an even more imperative way, in that it is, as other, and from the other, the language of our language. How then does one assume this responsibility, this capital duty [*devoir*]?

---

*Goût de fin, taste for the end, is a play on *fin goût*—fine or refined taste.—Trans.

How does one respond? And above all, how does one assume a responsibility that announces itself as contradictory because it inscribes us from the very beginning of the game into a kind of necessarily double obligation, a *double bind*? The injunction in effect divides us; it puts us always at fault or in default since it doubles the *il faut,* the *it is necessary:* it is necessary to make ourselves the guardians of an idea of Europe, of a difference of Europe, *but* of a Europe that consists precisely in not closing itself off in its own identity and in advancing itself in an exemplary way toward what it is not, toward the other heading or the heading of the other, indeed—and this is perhaps something else altogether—toward the other *of* the heading, which would be the beyond of this modern tradition, another border structure, another shore.

To be faithfully responsible *for* this memory, and thus to respond rigorously to this double injunction: will this have to consist in repeating or in breaking with, in continuing or in opposing? Or indeed in attempting to

invent another gesture, an epic *gesture** in truth,
that presupposes memory precisely in order
to assign identity from alterity, from the
other heading and the other of the heading,
from a completely other shore?

This last hypothesis, the one toward
which I will prefer to orient myself, is not
only a hypothesis or a call, a call toward that
which is given at the same time as contradictory or impossible. No, I believe that *this is
taking place now.* (But it is also necessary, for
this, to begin to think that this "now" would
be neither present, nor current, nor the present of some current event.) Not that it ar-
rives, that it happens or has already
happened, not that it is already *presently*
given. I believe, rather, that this event takes
place as that which comes, as that which
seeks or promises itself *today,* in Europe, the
today of a Europe whose borders are not
given—no more than its name, Europe being

---

*A play on *un geste,* a gesture, and *une geste,* a collection of
epic poems—as in the *chanson de geste.* "Epic gesture" is thus
a somewhat elliptical rendering of *une longue geste.*—Trans.

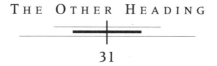
here only a *paleonymic* appellation. I believe that if there is any event today, it is taking place here, in this act of memory that consists in betraying a certain order of capital in order to be faithful to the other heading and to the other of the heading. And this is happening at a moment for which the word *crisis*, the crisis of Europe or the crisis of spirit, is perhaps no longer appropriate.

The coming to awareness, the reflection by which, in regaining consciousness, one again finds one's "direction" [*sens*: meaning] (*Selbstbesinnung*),* this recovery of European cultural identity as *capital* discourse, this moment of awakening, of sounding the alarm, has always been deployed in the tradition of modernity at the moment and as the very moment of what was called *crisis*. This is the moment of decision, the moment of *krinein*, the dramatic instant of a decision that is still impossible and suspended, imminent and

---

*Literally "self-contemplation," *Selbstbesinnung* is a common term in Protestant religious texts and in German Idealism.—Trans.

threatening. The crisis of Europe as the crisis of spirit: they all say this at the moment when the limits and contours, the *eidos,* the ends and confines, the finitude of Europe, are beginning to emerge; that is to say, when the capital of infinity and universality, which is to be found in reserve within the idiom of these limits, finds itself encroached upon or in danger.

We will later ask ourselves what this threat consists of *today.* This critical moment can take several forms, all of which, in spite of their sometimes serious differences, specify a fundamentally analogous "logic." There was, for example, the form of the Hegelian moment wherein European discourse coincided with spirit's return to itself in Absolute Knowledge, at this "end-of-history" that today can give rise to the prating eloquence of a White House advisor [this was, let me recall, before what is known as the Gulf War: is the Gulf the Headland or the Heading, or is it the negative or the other of the Heading?] when he announces with great media fanfare "the end-of-history." This, if one were to be-

lieve him, because the essentially European model of the market economy, of liberal, parliamentary, and capitalist democracies, would be about to become a universally recognized model, all the nation states of the planet preparing themselves to join us at the head of the pack, right at the forefront [*cap*], at the capital point [*pointe*] of advanced democracies, there where capital is on the cutting edge of progress [*à la pointe du progrès*].

There was also the Husserlian form of the "crisis of European sciences" or the "crisis of European humanity": the teleology that guides the analysis of history and the very history of this crisis, of the recovery of the transcendental theme in and since Descartes, is guided by the idea of a transcendental community, the subjectivity of a "we" for which Europe would be at once the name and the exemplary figure. This transcendental teleology would have, from the origin of philosophy, shown the way, indicated the heading.

There at the same time, and what a time, in 1935–1936, the Heideggerian discourse, which deplored the *Entmachtung*

of spirit. The impotence, the becoming-impotent of spirit, that which violently deprives spirit of its potency, is nothing other than the destitution (*Entmachtung*) of the European West.* Even though he is opposed to transcendental sub-objectivism, or to the Cartesian-Husserlian tradition as its symptom, Heidegger nevertheless calls for thinking the essential danger as the danger *of spirit,* and spirit as something of the European West, there at the oppressed center of a vice, in the *Mitte* of Europe, between America and Russia.[4]

At the same time, I mean between the two world wars, from 1919–1939, Valéry defines *the crisis of spirit* as the crisis of Europe, of European identity, and more precisely of European culture. Having chosen for today the configured direction of the heading and of capital, I will pause for a while in the vicinity of Valéry, and for several reasons, all of

---

*On the translation of *Entmachtung* as destitution, cf. Derrida's *Of Spirit,* trans. Geoffrey Bennington and Rachel Bowlby (Chicago: University of Chicago Press, 1989), pp. 59ff.—Trans.

which touch upon the capital point [*la pointe*], upon the point [*le point*] of capital.*

Valéry is a Mediterranean spirit. When speaking of the Mediterranean lake, what are we naming? Like all the names we are invoking, like all names in general, these designate at once a limit, a negative limit, and a chance. For perhaps responsibility consists in making of the name recalled, of the memory of the name, of the idiomatic limit, a chance, that is, an opening of identity to its very future. All Valéry's works are those of a European from the Greco-Roman Mediterranean world, close to Italy in his birth and his death: I emphasize this no doubt because we are here, today, in Turin, in a Latin place of the northern Mediterranean. But this Mediterranean shore also interests me—coming as I do from the other shore if not from the other heading (from a shore that is principally neither French, nor European, nor

---

*The feminine *la pointe* refers, among other things, to a head, end, tip, point, or headland, while the masculine *le point* refers to a place, position, or mark.—Trans.

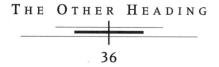
Latin, nor Christian)—because of this word "capital," which slowly leads me toward the most hesitant, trembling, and divided point of my remarks, a point at once undecidable and decided.

This word "capital" capitalizes in effect, in the body of the idiom, and, if I may say this, in the same body, two genres of questions. More precisely: *a question in two genres, with two genders* [*à deux genres*].

1. It comes down first *to the feminine, in the feminine:* the question of *la capitale.* We are far from being able to avoid it today. Are there grounds for this, is there from now on *a place* for a capital of European culture? Can one project a center, at least a symbolic center, at the heart of this Europe that has considered itself for so long to be the capital of humanity or of the planet and that would renounce this role today, some believe, only at the moment when the fable of a planetarization of the European model still seems quite plausible? In this form, the question may seem crude and outdated. Surely, there will be no official capital of European culture. No one is consider-

ing this and no one would accept it. But the ineluctable question of the capital does not disappear for all that. It now signals toward struggles over cultural hegemony. Through the established and traditionally dominant powers of certain idioms, of certain culture industries, through the extraordinary growth of new media, newspapers, and publishers, through the university and through techno-scientific powers, through new "capillarities," competitions—sometimes silent but always fierce—have broken out. This now happens according to new modes, in a fast-changing situation where the centralizing pulsions do not always go through states. (For it can even happen, and one can cautiously hope for this, that in certain cases the old state structures help us to fight against private and transnational empires.) Let us think about the novelty of these modes of cultural domination as if they themselves were those geographico-political domains that have become the objects of everyone's desire since *perestroika,* the destruction of the Berlin Wall, all the movements of "democra-

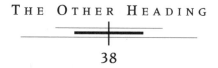
tization,'' and all the more or less potential currents that run through Europe: it is then that we witness the resurgence of the question of the capital, that is, the question of hegemonic centrality. The fact that this center can no longer be fixed in the traditional form of the metropolis no doubt obliges us to acknowledge what is happening today to the city. But this does not do away with all reference to capitals. Quite the contrary. The reference must be translated and displaced within a problematic that is profoundly transformed by techno-scientific and techno-economic givens. These givens also affect, among other things, the production, transmission, structure, and effects of the very discourses in which one tries to formalize this problematic, just as they affect the figure of those who produce or publicly hold these discourses—namely, ourselves, or those who in the past were so easily called ''intellectuals.''

First tension, first contradiction, double injunction: *on the one hand,* European cultural identity cannot be dispersed (and when I say ''cannot,'' this should also be taken as ''must

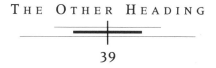
not"—and this double state of affairs is at the heart of the difficulty). It cannot and must not be dispersed into a myriad of provinces, into a multiplicity of self-enclosed idioms or petty little nationalisms, each one jealous and untranslatable. It cannot and must not renounce places of great circulation or heavy traffic, the great avenues or thoroughfares of translation and communication, and thus, of mediatization. But, *on the other hand,* it cannot and must not accept the capital of a centralizing authority that, by means of trans-European cultural mechanisms, by means of publishing, journalistic, and academic concentrations—be they state-run or not—would control and standardize, subjecting artistic discourses and practices to a grid of intelligibility, to philosophical or aesthetic norms, to channels of immediate and efficient communication, to the pursuit of ratings and commercial profitability. For by reconstituting places of an easy consensus, places of a demagogical and "salable" consensus, through mobile, omnipresent, and extremely rapid media networks, by thus immediately crossing every border, such

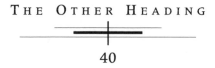
normalization would establish a cultural capital at any place and at all times. It would establish a hegemonic center, the power center or power station [*la centrale*], the media center or central switchboard [*le central*] of the new *imperium: remote control* as one says in English for the TV, a ubiquitous tele-command, quasi-immediate and absolute. One no longer needs to link the cultural capital to a metropolis, to a site or geographico-political city. Yet the question of the capital remains completely intact, and indeed even more intrusive in that its "politics"—which perhaps no longer constitute anything deserving this name—are no longer linked to the *polis* (city, town, acropolis, neighborhood), to the traditional concept of *politeia* or *res publica*. We are perhaps moving into a zone or topology that will be called neither political nor apolitical but, to make cautious use of an old word for new concepts, "quasi-political." This is a quasi-quotation from Valéry—once again—who gave as a general title for a series of texts devoted to the crisis of spirit as the crisis of Europe: "Quasi-Political Essays."

Neither monopoly nor dispersion, therefore. This is, of course, an aporia, and we must not hide it from ourselves. I will even venture to say that ethics, politics, and responsibility, *if there are any,* will only ever have begun with the experience and experiment of the aporia. When the path is clear and given, when a certain knowledge opens up the way in advance, the decision is already made, it might as well be said that there is none to make: irresponsibly, and in good conscience, one simply applies or implements a program. Perhaps, and this would be the objection, one never escapes the program. In that case, one must acknowledge this and stop talking with authority about moral or political responsibility. The condition of possibility of this thing called responsibility is a certain *experience and experiment of the possibility of the impossible: the testing of the aporia* from which one may invent the only *possible invention, the impossible invention.*[5]

The aporia here takes the logical form of a contradiction. A contradiction that is all the more serious in that, if these movements of

"democratization" have accelerated, it is to a large extent thanks to this new techno-media power, to this penetrating, rapid, and irresistible circulation of images, ideas, and models, thanks to this extreme *capillarity* of discourses. Capillarity: one need not split hairs to recognize in this word all the lines that interest us at this moment, at this point [*point*], at the point or end [*pointe*] where their fineness becomes microscopic; *cabled, targeted* [*cablée, ciblée*], as close as possible to the head and to the headman [*chef*], that is circulation, communication, an almost immediate irrigation. Such capillarity crosses not only national borders. For we know that a totalitarian system can no longer effectively fight against an internal telephone network once its density has exceeded a certain threshold, thereby becoming uncontrollable. Indeed, no "modern" society (and modernity is an imperative for totalitarianism) can refuse for very long to develop the technico-economico-scientific services of the telephone—which is to say, the "democratic" places of connection appropriate to operating its own destruction. The tele-

phone thus becomes, for totalitarianism, the invisible prefiguration and the imperious prescription of its own ruin. For the telephone no longer leaves in place the limit between public and private, assuming that such a limit was ever rigorous. The telephone inaugurates the formation of a *public opinion* there where the usual conditions of "publicity"*—the "written" or "spoken" press, publishing in all its forms—are denied access to it. In short, telephone lines—and soon the videophone—are inseparable from the great channels of communication, from television or teleprinters. And if it is in the name of free and open discussion with a view to consensus, in the name of traditional democracy, that these avenues of media are opened up, it would be out of the question to fight against them. It would be anti-democratic to break up, marginalize, shut off, deny access, and disconnect.

---

*Derrida puts the word *publicité* in quotation marks because it means both "publicness" and, more commonly, publicity or advertising.—Trans.

Yet here as elsewhere, the injunction seems double and contradictory for whoever is concerned about European cultural identity: if it is necessary to make sure that a centralizing hegemony (the capital) not be reconstituted, it is also necessary, for all that, not to multiply the borders, i.e., the movements [*marches*] and margins [*marges*]. It is necessary not to cultivate for their own sake minority differences, untranslatable idiolects, national antagonisms, or the chauvinisms of idiom. Responsibility seems to consist today in renouncing neither of these two contradictory imperatives. One must therefore try to *invent* gestures, discourses, politico-institutional practices that inscribe the alliance of these two imperatives, of these two promises or contracts: the capital and the a-capital, the other of the capital. That is not easy. It is even impossible to conceive of a responsibility that consists in being responsible *for* two laws, or that consists in responding *to* two contradictory injunctions. No doubt. But there is no responsibility that is not the experience and experiment of the im-

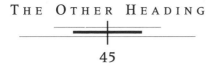
possible. As we said just a moment ago, when a responsibility is exercised in the order of the possible, it simply follows a direction and elaborates a program. It makes of action the applied consequence, the simple application of a knowledge or know-how. It makes of ethics and politics a technology. No longer of the order of practical reason or decision, it begins to be irresponsible. Taking a few shortcuts, economizing on mediations, it would seem that European cultural identity, like identity or identification in general, if it must be equal *to itself and to the other,* up to the measure of its own immeasurable difference "with itself," belongs, therefore *must* belong, to this *experience and experiment of the impossible.* Nevertheless, one will always be able *de jure* to ask what an ethics or a politics that measures responsibility only by the rule of the impossible can be: as if doing only what were possible amounted to abandoning the ethical and political realms, or as if, inversely, in order to take an authentic responsibility it were necessary to limit oneself to impossible, impractical, and inapplicable

decisions. If the two terms of such an alternative translate at once an unsolvable contradiction and an unequivocal seriousness, the aporia is reflected or capitalized *in abyss* and requires more than ever thinking differently, or thinking at last, what is announced here in the enigmatic form of the "possible" (of the possibility—itself impossible—of the impossible, etc.).

It is in this direction (if one could still say and identify it) that we asked in what new terms, and according to what other topology, the question of the *place* for a capital of European culture would be asked today, the question of at least a symbolic place: a place that would be neither strictly political (linked to the establishing of some state or parliamentary institution), nor the center of economic or administrative decision making, nor a city chosen for its geographical location, for the size of its airport or for a hotel infrastructure large enough to meet the demands of a European Parliament (this is the well-known competition between Brussels and Strasbourg). Whether directly or not, the hypothesis of

this capital always concerns language, not only the predominance of a national language, tongue, or idiom, but the predominance of a *concept* of the tongue or of language, a certain idea of the idiom that is being put to work.

Refraining from giving any examples, let us emphasize for the moment a generality: in this struggle for control over culture, in this strategy that tries to organize cultural identity around a capital that is all the more powerful for being mobile, that is, European in a hyper- or supra-national sense, national hegemony is not claimed—today no more than ever—in the name of an empirical superiority, which is to say, a simple particularity. That is why nationalism, national affirmation, as an essentially modern phenomenon, is always a philosopheme. National hegemony *presents itself,* claims itself. It claims to justify itself in the name of a privilege in responsibility and in the memory of the universal and, thus, of the transnational—indeed of the trans-European—and, finally, of the transcendental or ontological. The logical

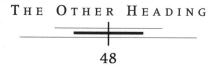
schema of this argument, the backbone of this national self-affirmation, the nuclear statement of the national "ego" or "subject," is, to put it quite dryly: "I am (we are) all the more national for being European, all the more European for being trans-European and international; no one is more cosmopolitan and authentically universal than the one, than this 'we,' who is speaking to you." Nationalism and cosmopolitanism have always gotten along well together, as paradoxical as this may seem. Since the time of Fichte, numerous examples might attest to this. In the logic of this "capitalistic" and cosmopolitical discourse, what is proper to a particular nation or idiom would be to be a heading for Europe; and what is proper to Europe would be, analogically, to advance itself as a heading for the universal essence of humanity. *To advance itself,* that is the word, for it capitalizes most of the figures we have been observing here. To advance oneself is, certainly, to *present oneself,* to introduce or show oneself, thus to identify and name oneself. To advance oneself is also to rush out ahead, looking in

front of oneself ("Europe looks naturally to-
ward the West"), to anticipate, to go on
ahead, to launch oneself onto the sea or into
adventure, to take the lead in taking the initiative, and sometimes even to go on the of-
fensive. To advance (oneself) is also to take
risks, to stick one's neck out, sometimes to
overestimate one's strengths, to make
hypotheses, to sniff things out precisely there
where one no longer sees (the nose, the peninsula, Cape Cyrano). Europe takes itself to
be a promontory, an advance—the avant-
garde of geography and history. It advances
and promotes itself as an advance, and it will
have never ceased to make advances on the
other: to induce, seduce, produce, and con-
duce, to spread out, to cultivate, to love or to
violate, to love to violate, to colonize, and to
colonize itself.

Since I am speaking French, and so as not
to trigger any inter-national *polemos,* I will
cite the language most common to *all* the majorities of the French Republic. Without exception, they claim for France, which is to
say, of course, for Paris,[6] for the capital of all

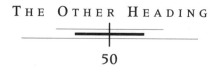
revolutions and for the Paris of today, the role of the avant-garde, for example, in the idea of democratic culture, that is, quite simply, of free culture itself, which is founded on an idea of human rights [*droits*], on an idea of international law [*droit*]. No matter what the English say today, France would have invented these human rights, among which is the *"freedom of thought,"* which means "in common usage," and I am again citing Valéry, *"freedom to publish,* or else *freedom to teach."*[7]

I am here referring, for example, to a certain official document coming out of the Ministry of Foreign Affairs (the State Secretary of International Cultural Relations). This sophisticated text defines in a competent and convincing way what is called the "European cultural construction." To do this, it first puts in exergue a sentence from the "Congress on European Cultural Space" (Stuttgart, June 18, 1988), which associates the themes of conquest, imposition, and spirit [*esprit*]. (*"Esprit"* is, moreover, next to *"Brite"* and "Race" [the English word that also means "contest"

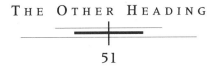
or "competition"], the proper name for one of the European Community's programs for technological development.) "There is no political ambition that is not preceded by a *conquest of spirit(s):** it is the task of *culture* to *impose* the feeling of unity, of European solidarity" (my emphasis). The opposite page underscores "the determining role" that France plays in the "collective coming to awareness." This same document cites in its exergue a communiqué of the French Cabinet, which states that "French culture" acts "by teaching others to look to France as a creative country that is helping to build modernity." More precisely, it states (and I emphasize here the language of *response, responsibility,* and *today*), that "[France, French culture] is *responsible* for *today,* and this is what is expected of her." French cultural identity would thus be *responsible* for the European *today* and, thus, as always, for the

---

*For the sake of consistency and in light of Derrida's own comments in *Of Spirit,* we have translated *esprit* as spirit throughout, even though it might, as here, have been more naturally translated as "mind."—Trans.

trans-European, over-European [*outre-Européen*] *today*. It would be responsible for the universe: and for human rights and international law—which logically presupposes that it is the first to denounce divergences between the principle of these rights (whose reaffirmation must be and can only be unconditional) and the concrete conditions of their implementation, the determined limits of their representation, the abuses of or inequalities in their application as a result of certain interests, monopolies, or existing hegemonies. The task is always at once urgent and infinite. One cannot but be *unequal* to it, but there are many ways to determine, interpret, or "govern" this *inadequation:* that is what politics is all about, and always about, *today.* And France assigns herself this *exemplary* task according to the principle of the discourse that we just cited ("[France] is responsible for today, and this is what is expected of her"). Identity would thus be instituted in responsibility, which is to say—and we will come back to this—in a certain experience and experiment of the response

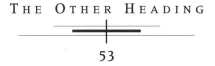
that here bears the whole enigma. What is it "to respond"? To respond to? To be responsible for? To respond for? To respond, be responsible, before?

The same text also recalls that France must "conserve its avant-garde position." "Avant-garde": the word is always so "attractive," whether or not it be extracted from its strategico-military code (*promos*) as projectile or missile. This word capitalizes upon the figurehead, the figure of prowess, the figure on or of the prow, of the phallic point advanced like a beak, like a quill, or like the nib of a pen—the shape of the headland or the cape, therefore, *and* of the *guard* or of memory. It adds the value of a proposed or advanced initiative to that of recollection: the responsibility of the guardian, the vocation of a remembrance that takes it upon itself to take the initiative, especially when it is in advance a matter of guarding, of anticipating in order to "conserve," as the official text says, an "avant-garde position," and thus of conserving itself as the avant-garde that advances in order to conserve what is its due, namely,

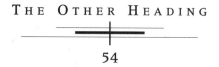
venturing forth in order to conserve what is once again its due, namely, an "avant-garde position"—of course.

This is state talk, but vigilance must be exercised not only in regard to state discourses. The best intentioned of European projects, those that are quite apparently and explicitly pluralistic, democratic, and tolerant, may try, in this lovely competition for the "conquest of spirit(s)," to impose the homogeneity of a medium, of discursive norms and models.

This can happen, surely, through newspaper or magazine consortiums, through powerful European publishing enterprises. There is a multiplication of such projects today, and we can be happy about this, provided our attention does not lapse. For it is necessary that we learn to detect, in order then to resist, new forms of cultural takeover. This can also happen through a new university space, and especially through a philosophical discourse. Under the pretext of pleading for transparency (along with "consensus," "transparency" is one of the master words of the

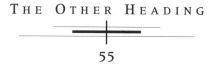
"cultural" discourse I just mentioned), for the univocity of democratic discussion, for communication in public space, for "communicative action," such a discourse tends to impose a model of language that is supposedly favorable to this communication. Claiming to speak in the name of intelligibility, good sense, common sense, or the democratic ethic, this discourse tends, by means of these very things, and as if naturally, to discredit anything that complicates this model. It tends to suspect or repress anything that bends, overdetermines, or even questions, in theory or in practice, this idea of language. With this concern, among others, in mind, it would be necessary to study certain rhetorical norms that dominate analytic philosophy or what is called in Frankfurt "transcendental pragmatics." These models coincide with certain institutional powers that are not restricted to England and Germany. Under these or other names, they are present and powerful elsewhere, including France. It is a question here of a common space, common, as an implicit contract might be, to the press,

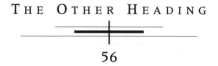
to the publishing industry, to the media, and to the university, to the philosophy of the university and to philosophy in the university.

2. That was the question of the heading [*cap*] as the question of *la capitale.* One can already see how it can be linked to a new question of *le capital,* to the question of what links capital to the theme of European identity. To say it all too quickly, I am thinking about the necessity for a new culture, one that would invent another way of reading and analyzing *Capital,* both Marx's book and capital in general; a new way of taking capital into account while avoiding not only the frightening totalitarian dogmatism that some of us have known how to resist up until now, *but also, and simultaneously,* the counter-dogmatism that is setting in today, (on the) left and (on the) right, exploiting a new situation, interrogating it to the point of banning the word "capital," indeed even the critique of certain effects of capital or of the "market" as the evil remnants of the old dogmatism. Is it not necessary to have the courage

and lucidity for a *new* critique of the *new* effects of capital (within unprecedented techno-social structures)? Is not this responsibility incumbent upon *us,* most particularly upon those who never gave in to a certain Marxist intimidation? Just as it is necessary to analyze and earnestly address—and this is the whole problem of ethico-political responsibility—the disparities between law, ethics, and politics, or between the unconditional idea of law (be it of men or of states) and the concrete conditions of its implementation, between the structurally universalist pretention of these regulative ideas and the essence or European origin of this idea of law (etc.), is it not also necessary to resist with vigilance the neo-capitalist exploitation of the breakdown of an anti-capitalist dogmatism in those states that had incorporated it?

For the moment, we must focus our attention on the word "capital," or more precisely on the tenor of its idiom, in order to justify the reference to Valéry. Like the vocable "cap," but also like the "culture" words, those from *"colo,"* as in "colony" and "colo-

nization," and like "civilization," etc., the word "capital" is a Latin word. The semantic accumulation that we are now highlighting organizes a polysemy around the central reserve, itself a capital reserve, of an idiom. By giving cause to remark upon this language, the language in which even this right here is being spoken, or at least predominantly so, we are focusing attention upon the critical stakes: the question of idioms and translation. What philosophy of translation will dominate in Europe? In a Europe that from now on should avoid both the nationalistic tensions of linguistic difference and the violent homogenization of languages through the neutrality of a translating medium that would claim to be transparent, metalinguistic, and universal?

I remember that last year, in this very place, a name was chosen for an important European newspaper. Through the diffusive presence of five already existing and influential newspapers, this new newspaper would link five capitals of European culture (Turin, *L'Indice*; Madrid, *El Pais*; Paris, *Le Monde*;

Frankfurt, *Frankfurter Allgemeine Zeitung;* and London, *Times Literary Supplement).** There would be much to say about the necessity of so many analogous projects. Let us consider only the title chosen for this newspaper. It is a Latin title, and it was accepted by the English as well as the Germans. The newspaper is called *Liber* (*Revue européenne des livres*). Those in charge of the newspaper are quite attached—and they are entitled to be so—to this name's rich polysemy, since they recall its elliptical economy in each issue. This polysemy gathers the homonyms and derivations at play in the lexical roots of a rich Latin soil: "(1) *Liber, era, erum:* free (socially), of free birth, emancipated, independent, free (morally); absolute, unbridled, free from restraint. (2) *Liber, eri:* the name of Bacchus, wine. (3) *Liber, bri:* the inner bark of a tree used for writing; a book, writing, treatise, or play; a collection, catalogue, or newspaper."

---

*The reader will have noticed that the preface makes no mention of the *Times Literary Supplement.* They apparently decided in the end not to participate in the project.—Trans.

By playing so seriously, and with a calcu-
lated irony, at recalling the memory of the
language at the very moment of reawakening
this identity of European culture, by pretend-
ing to gather this memory around freedom,
the grape vine, and the book, one renews an
alliance and reaffirms *at the same time* a
Europeo-Mediterranean idiom. If I added the
untranslatable homophone *"libère,"* "liberate
yourself, you and the others" [*libère-toi, toi et
les autres*], namely, a command in the familiar
form [*un ordre qui tutoie*],* a familiar imperative in the form of a jussive** speech act that
is possible only in the idiom of "my" own
language, you would be even more sensitive
to the problem that I wish to raise. It concerns an irreducible experience of language,
that which *links* it to the *liaison,* to commit-
ment, to the command or to the promise: before and beyond all theoretico-constatives,
opening, embracing, or including them,

---

*Derrida is referring to the familiar form of address—the
"tu" of the second person singular.—Trans.

**A common term in speech act theory. From the Latin
jubeo—to order or command.—Trans.

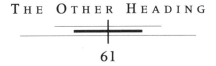
there is the affirmation of language, the "I am addressing you, and I commit myself, in this language here; listen how I speak in my language, me, and you can speak to me in your language; we must hear each other, we must get along" [*nous devons nous entendre*]. This affirmation defies all metalanguage, even if it produces, and precisely for this, by this even, the effects of metalanguage.

Why speak today, only today, and why name today the "today" in the margins of Valéry? If this could be rigorously justified, which I doubt, it would be because of that which, in a certain text of Valéry, bears the marks of an urgency, or, more properly, an *imminence.* It is an imminence whose repetition we seem to be living, but whose irreducible singularity we should now, in an even more imperative way, recover from against the backdrop of analogy and resemblance. In what does our experience of imminence differ *today*? And, to sketch out the analysis in advance, how, in Valéry's time, did an imminence come on the scene that so much *resembles* our own, to the point where we wrongly

and too precipitately borrow from it so many discursive schema?

The Freedom of Spirit appears in 1939, on the eve of the war. Valéry recalls the *imminence* of a tremor that was not only going to reduce to rubble—among other things—what was called Europe. It was also going to destroy Europe in the name of an idea of Europe, of a Young Europe that attempted to assure its hegemony. The "Western democratic" nations, in their turn, and in the name of another idea of Europe, prevented a certain European unification by destroying nazism, allied as they were for a limited but decisive time to the Soviet Union. In 1939, the imminence was not only a terrifying cultural configuration of Europe constructed through a succession of exclusions, annexations, and exterminations. It was also the imminence of a war and a victory in the wake of which a partitioning of European culture was going to be fixed for the time of a quasi-naturalization of borders, the time in which the intellectuals of my generation have lived most of their adult lives. With the destruction of the Berlin Wall

and the unification of Germany in sight, with
a *perestroika* that is still uncertain, with all the
diverse movements of "democratization,"
and with all the legitimate but sometimes am-
biguous aspirations for national sovereignty,
there is in *today's* day and age the reopening
and denaturalization of these monstrous par-
titions. There is *today* the same feeling of imminence, of hope and of danger, of anxiety
before the possibility of other wars with
unknown forms, the return to old forms of
religious fanaticism, nationalism, or racism.
There is the greatest uncertainty concerning
the borders of Europe itself, its geographico-
political borders (in the center, to the east and
to the west, to the north and to the south), its
"spiritual" borders (around the idea of philosophy, reason, monotheism, Jewish, Greek,
Christian [Catholic, Protestant, Orthodox],
and Islamic memories, around Jerusalem, a
Jerusalem itself divided, torn apart, around
Athens, Rome, Moscow, Paris, and it is necessary to add, "etc.," and it is necessary to divide yet again each of these names with the
most respectful persistence).

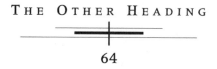
In *The Freedom of Spirit,* this text of immi-
nence whose stakes are indeed the destiny of
European culture, Valéry makes a determining appeal to the word *capital,* precisely in
order to define culture—and the Mediterranean. He evokes navigation, exchange, this
"same ship" that carried "merchandise and
gods . . . ideas and methods."

> That is how all that wealth came into being,
> to which our culture owes practically every-
> thing, at least in its origins; I may say that
> the Mediterranean has been a veritable *ma-
> chine for making civilization.* And in creating
> trade, it necessarily created *freedom of the
> spirit.* On the shores of the Mediterranean,
> then, *spirit, culture, and trade* are found to-
> gether (II, p. 1086 [*History and Politics,*
> p. 196]).

After having extended the principle of
this analysis to the cities along the Rhine (Ba-
sel, Strasbourg, Cologne), to the harbors of
the Hanse, which are also "strategic positions
of spirit," secured by the alliance of financial
institutions, the arts, and the printing indus-

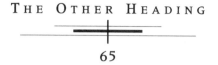
try, Valéry puts to work the regulated poly-
semy of the word "capital." This word
compounds interests, it would seem; it en-
riches with surplus value the significations of
memory, cultural accumulation, and economic or fiduciary value. Valéry assumes the
rhetoric of these tropes, the different figures
of capital referring to each other to the point
where one cannot nail them down into the
propriety of a literal meaning. But this non-
literality does not exclude hierarchy; it does
not put the whole semantic series on the
same level.[8]

What is the most interesting moment in
this semantic or rhetorical capitalization of
the values of "capital"? It is, it seems to me,
when the *regional* or *particular* necessity of capital produces or calls for the always threatened
production of the *universal*. European culture
is in danger when this *ideal* universality, the
very ideality of the universal as the production of capital, finds itself threatened:

Culture, civilization are rather vague terms
that it may be amusing to distinguish, con-

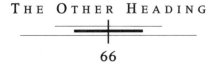
trast, or combine. I shall not dwell on them. For myself, as I have told you, they are a kind of capital that grows and can be used and accumulated, can increase and diminish like all the imaginable kinds of capital—the best known of which is, of course, what we call *our body* . . . (II, p. 1089 [*History and Politics*, p. 200]; Valéry's emphasis).

"Like all the imaginable kinds of capital": this analogical series is recalled in order to justify the lexicon of capital and the rhetoric thereby induced. And if I in turn insist on "our body," already emphasized by Valéry as in the end the best-*known*, the most familiar, capital, the one that gives capital its most literal or most proper meaning, thus gathering itself, as we have already seen, as close as possible to the head or to the heading, it is in order to remark that the body—as in what is called the proper body [*corps propre*], "our body," our *sexed* body or our body divided by sexual difference—remains one of the unavoidable sites of the problem. Through it also runs the question of the tongue, of language, of the idiom, and of the heading.

Valéry's diagnosis is the examination of a crisis, of the crisis *par excellence*, if one can say this, the crisis that endangers capital as cultural capital. "I say that our cultural capital is in peril." Like a doctor, Valéry analyzes the symptom of the "fever." He locates the illness in the very structure of capital. For capital presupposes the reality of the thing, that is, material culture, of course, but also human existence. The Valéryian rhetoric is here at once cultural, economic, technical, scientific, and military—i.e., strategic:

> Of what is the capital we call *Culture or Civilization* composed? In the first place, it is composed of *things,* material objects—books, pictures, instruments, etc.—having the probable lifespan, the fragility, and the precariousness of *things.* But this is not enough—any more than an ingot of gold, an acre of good land, or a machine can be capital unless there are men *who need them* and *know how to use them.* Note these two conditions. If the material of culture is to become capital, there must also be men who need and know how to use it—that is, men

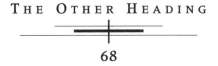
who have a thirst for knowledge and for the power of inner transformation, for the creations of their sensibility; and who, moreover, know how to acquire or exercise the habits, the intellectual discipline, the conventions and methods needed to exploit the arsenal of documents and instruments accumulated over the centuries.

I say that our cultural capital is in peril (II, pp. 1089–90, [*History and Politics,* pp. 200–201]).

The language of memory (putting into reserve, into the archive, documentation, accumulation) thus intersects the economic as well as the techno-scientific language of polemology (''knowledge,'' ''instruments,'' "power," "arsenal," etc.). The peril or danger that lies in wait for capital essentially threatens the "ideality" of capital: our "ideal capital," says Valéry. Ideality stems from that which in capitalization de-limits itself, that which exceeds the borders of sensible empiricity or of particularity in general in order to open onto the infinite and give rise to the universal. The maxim of maximization,

which, as we have seen, is nothing other than spirit itself, assigns to European man his essence ("All these maxima taken together are Europe").

We are quite familiar with the program of this logic—or this *analogic*. We could formalize it, experts that we are in such things, we, the old European philosophers. It is a logic, logic itself, that I do not wish to criticize here. I would even be ready to subscribe to it, but with one hand only, for I keep another to write or look for something else, perhaps outside Europe. Not only in order to look—in the way of research, analysis, knowledge, and philosophy—for what is already found outside Europe, but not to close off in advance a border to the future, to the to-come [*à-venir*] of the *event,* to that which *comes* [*vient*], which comes perhaps and perhaps comes from a completely other shore.

According to the capital logic that we see confirmed here, what threatens European identity would not essentially threaten Europe but, in Spirit, the universality for which Europe is responsible, of which it is the re-

serve, *le capital* or *la capitale*. What puts cultural capital as *ideal capital* into a state of crisis ("I have witnessed the gradual dying out of men of the greatest value for their contribution to our ideal capital . . . ") is the disappearance of these men who "knew how to read—a virtue now lost," these men who "knew . . . how to hear, and even how to listen," who "knew how to see," "to read, hear, or see again"—in a word, these men also capable of repetition and memory, prepared to respond, to respond *before,* to be responsible *for* and to respond *to* what they had heard, seen, read, and known for the first time. Through this responsible memory, what was constituted as "solid value" (Valéry emphasizes these two words) produced at the same time an absolute surplus value, namely, the increase of a universal capital: " . . . whatever they wished to read, hear, or see again was, by recapitulation, turned into a *solid value.* And the world's wealth was thus increased" (II, p. 1091 [*History and Politics,* pp. 201–202]).

Having approved this discourse while

looking elsewhere, I would like to precipi-
tate my conclusion; for precipitation is also
that movement of the head [*chef*] that propels
us headlong. It is indeed a question of this
capital paradox of universality. In it intersect
all the antinomies for which we seem to
have at our disposal no rule or general solution. We *have*, we *must* have, only the thank-
less aridity of an abstract axiom, namely,
that the experience and experiment of identity or of cultural identification can only be
the endurance of these antinomies. When
we say, "it seems that we do not have at our
disposal any rule or general solution," *is it*
not *necessary* in effect to infer or understand
by this, "*it is necessary* [*il faut*] that we do not
have them at our disposal"? Not only "it is
indeed necessary" [*il faut bien*], but "it need
be" [*il le faut*] absolutely, and this impover-
ished exposition is the negative form of the
imperative in which a responsibility, *if there
is any*, retains a chance of being affirmed. To
have at one's disposal, already in advance,
the generality of a rule [*règle*] as a solution to
the antinomy (that is, to the *double contradic-*

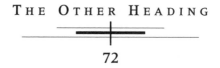
tory law and not to the opposition between the law and its other), to have it at one's disposal as a given potency or science, as a *knowledge* and a *power* that would precede, in order to settle [*régler*] it, the singularity of each decision, each judgment, each experience of responsibility, to treat each of these as if they were a case—this would be the surest, the most reassuring definition of *responsibility as irresponsibility,* of ethics confused with juridical calculation, of a politics organized within techno-science. Any invention of the new that would not go through the endurance of the antinomy would be a dangerous mystification, immorality *plus* good conscience, and sometimes good conscience *as* immorality.

The value of universality here capitalizes all the antinomies, for it must be linked to the value of *exemplarity* that inscribes the universal in the proper body of a singularity, of an idiom or a culture, whether this singularity be individual, social, national, state, federal, confederal, or not. Whether it takes a national form or not, a refined, hospitable or

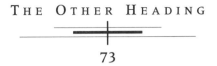
aggressively xenophobic form or not, the self-affirmation of an identity always claims to be responding to the call or assignation of the universal. There are no exceptions to this law. No cultural identity presents itself as the opaque body of an untranslatable idiom, but always, on the contrary, as the irreplaceable *inscription* of the universal in the singular, the *unique testimony* to the human essence and to what is proper to man. Each time, it has to do with the discourse of *responsibility:* I have, the unique "I" has, the responsibility of testifying for universality. Each time, the exemplarity of the example is unique. That is why it can be put into a series and formalized into a law. Among all the possible examples, I will cite, yet again, only Valéry's, since I find it just as typical or archetypical as any other. Moreover, it has here, for me who is speaking to you, the advantage of accentuating in French what is most "ridiculous" and "fine"—those are Valéry's words—about Gallocentrism. We are still in the theater of imminence. It is 1939. Evoking what he calls the "title" of France, which is again to say its

capital, since the value of a title is that of a head, a hat, a heading, a capstone, or a capital, Valéry concludes an essay entitled *French Thought and Art*:

> I will end by summarizing for you in two words my personal impression of France: our special quality (sometimes our ridicule, but often our finest claim or title) is to believe and to feel that we are universal—by which I mean, *men of universality*. . . . Notice the paradox: to specialize in the sense of the universal.[9]

One will have noted that what is described here is not a truth or an essence, even less a certainty: it is Valéry's "personal impression," stated as such by him, an impression regarding a *belief* and a *feeling* ("to believe and to feel that we are universal"). But these subjective phenomena (belief, feeling, an impression concerning them by someone who then says "we") would be no less constitutive of the essential or constitutive traits of French consciousness in its "particularity." This paradox is even stranger

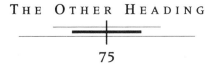
than Valéry could or wanted to think: the feeling of being "men of universality" is not reserved for the French. Not even, no doubt, for Europeans. Husserl said that insofar as the European philosopher is committed to universal reason, he is also the "functionary of mankind."*

From this paradox of the paradox, through the propagation of a fission reaction, all the propositions and injunctions are divided, the heading splits, the capital is de-identified: it is related to itself not only in gathering itself in the difference *with itself* and with the other heading, with the other shore of the heading, but in opening itself without being able any longer to gather itself. It opens itself, it has *already* begun to open itself, and *it is necessary* to take note of this, which means *to affirm in recalling,* and not simply to record or store up in the archives a necessity that is already at work any-

*From Husserl's *The Crisis of European Sciences and Transcendental Phenomenology: An Introduction to Phenomenological Philosophy,* tr. David Carr (Evanston: Northwestern University Press, 1970), p. 17.—Trans.

way. It has begun to open itself onto the *other shore of another heading,* even if it is an opposed heading, even if at war, and even if the opposition is internal. Yet it has at the same time, *and through this even,* begun to make out, to see coming, to hear or understand as well, the other *of* the heading in general. More radically still, with more gravity still—though this is the gravity of a light and imperceptible chance that is nothing other than the very experience and experiment of the other—it has begun to open itself, or rather to let itself open, or, better yet, to be affected with opening without opening *itself* onto an other, onto an other that the heading can no longer even relate to itself as *its* other, *the other with itself.*

Hence the *duty* to respond to the call of European memory, to recall what has been promised under the name Europe, to re-identify Europe—this *duty* is without common measure with all that is generally understood by the name duty, though it could be shown that all other duties perhaps presuppose it in silence.

This *duty* also dictates opening Europe, from the heading that is divided because it is also a shoreline: opening it onto that which is not, never was, and never will be Europe.

The *same duty* also dictates welcoming foreigners in order not only to integrate them but to recognize and accept their alterity: two concepts of hospitality that today divide our European and national consciousness.

The *same duty* dictates *criticizing* (''in-both-theory-and-in-practice,'' and relentlessly) a totalitarian dogmatism that, under the pretense of putting an end to capital, destroyed democracy and the European heritage. But it also dictates criticizing a religion of capital that institutes its dogmatism under new guises, which we must also learn to identify—for this is the future itself, and there will be none otherwise.

The *same duty* dictates cultivating the virtue of such *critique, of the critical idea, the critical tradition,* but also submitting it, beyond critique and questioning, to a deconstructive genealogy that thinks and exceeds it without yet compromising it.

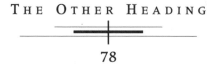
The *same duty* dictates assuming the European, and *uniquely* European, heritage of an idea of democracy, while also recognizing that this idea, like that of international law, is never simply given, that its status is not even that of a regulative idea in the Kantian sense, but rather something that remains to be thought and *to come* [*à venir*]: not something that is certain to happen tomorrow, not the democracy (national or international, state or trans-state) of the *future,* but a democracy that must have the structure of a promise—*and thus the memory of that which carries the future, the to-come, here and now.*

The *same duty* dictates respecting differences, idioms, minorities, singularities, but also the universality of formal law, the desire for translation, agreement and univocity, the law of the majority, opposition to racism, nationalism, and xenophobia.

The *same duty* demands tolerating and respecting all that is not placed under the authority of reason. It may have to do with faith, with different forms of faith. It may also have to do with certain thoughts,

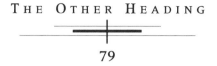
whether questioning or not, thoughts that, while attempting to think reason and the history of reason, necessarily exceed its order, without becoming, simply because of this, irrational, and much less irrationalist. For these thoughts may in fact also try to remain faithful to the ideal of the Enlightenment, the *Aufklärung,* the *Illuminismo,* while yet acknowledging its limits, in order to work on the Enlightenment of this time, this time that is ours—*today.* Today, today once more ("What are you going to do TODAY?").

This *same duty* surely calls for responsibility, for the responsibility to think, speak, and act in compliance with this double contradictory imperative—a contradiction that must not be only an apparent or illusory antinomy (not even a transcendental illusion in a Kantian type of dialectic) but must be effective and, *with experience, through experiment,* interminable. But it also calls for respecting whatever refuses a certain responsibility, for example, the responsibility to respond before any and every instituted tribunal. We know that it was in using the discourse of responsibility that

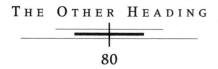
the most atrocious Zhdanovism* was able to be exercised against intellectuals accused of irresponsibility before Society or History, "represented" at that time, *presently,* by some determined, that is, present, state of society or history, which is simply to say, by some State.

I am going to stop because it is late. One could multiply the examples of this double duty. It would be necessary above all to discern the unprecedented forms that it is taking today in Europe. And not only to accept but to claim this putting to the test of the antinomy (in the forms, for example, of the double constraint, the undecidable, the performative contradiction, etc.). It would be necessary to recognize both the typical or recurring form and the inexhaustible singularization—without which there will never be any event, decision, responsibility, ethics, or politics. These conditions can only take a negative *form* (without X there would not be

---

*Andrei Alexandrovich Zhdanov (1896–1948) was an important Communist party leader who was responsible, under Stalin, for a program that censored "bourgeois deviationism" in literature and the arts.—Trans.

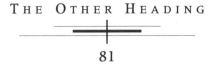
Y). One can be certain only of this negative form. As soon as it is converted into positive certainty ("on this condition, there will surely have been event, decision, responsibility, ethics, or politics"), one can be sure that one is beginning to be deceived, indeed beginning to deceive the other.

We are speaking here with names (event, decision, responsibility, ethics, politics—Europe!) of "things" that can only exceed (and *must* exceed) the order of theoretical determination, of knowledge, certainty, judgment, and of statements in the form of "this is that," in other words, more generally and essentially, the order of the *present* or of *presentation*. Each time they are reduced to what they must exceed, error, recklessness, the unthought, and irresponsibility are given the so very presentable face of good conscience. (And it is also necessary to say that the serious, unsmiling mask of a declared bad conscience often exhibits only a supplementary ruse; for good conscience has, by definition, inexhaustible resources, and one will always be able to exploit them.)

One last word. Like the fission reaction it propagates in our discourse, the paradox of the paradox should lead us to take the old name of Europe at once very seriously and cautiously, that is, to take it lightly, only in quotation marks, as the best paleonym, in a certain situation, for what we recall (to ourselves) or what we promise (ourselves). For the same reasons, I would use the word "capital" in a similar way: *la capitale* or *le capital.* And, naturally, the words "identity" and "culture."

I am European, I am no doubt a European intellectual, and I like to recall this, I like to recall this to myself, and why would I deny it? In the name of what? But I am not, nor do I feel, European *in every part,* that is, European through and through. By which I mean, by which I wish to say, or *must* say: I do not want to be and must not be European through and through, European *in every part.* Being a part, belonging as "fully a part," should be incompatible with belonging "in every part." My cultural identity, that in the name of which I speak, is not only European,

it is not identical to itself, and I am not "cultural" through and through, "cultural" in every part.

If, to conclude, I declared that I feel European *among other things,* would this be, in this very declaration, to be more or less European? Both, no doubt. Let the consequences be drawn from this. It is up to the others, in any case, and up to me *among them,* to decide.

CALL IT A DAY
FOR DEMOCRACY

*T*oday, what is public opinion?

—Today? The silhouette of a phantom, the haunting fear of democratic consciousness. The phantom has rights and powers, but how does one put a stop to contradictory demands? Why must parliamentary democracy protect itself from what in fact resembles the source of its legitimacy? Yes, you are right to specify: today, *in the light* of today, in today's *day* and age [*au jour*

This is the complete version of an interview (with Olivier Salvatori and Nicolas Weill) that was published in an abbreviated form in *Le Monde de la Révolution française*, no. 1 (monthly, January 1989).

d'aujourd'hui]. Concerning the *rhythm,* the *medium,* and first of all the *history* of public opinion, it has to do with the question of the *day* [*jour*].

1. Opinion lends to "public opinions" the vice or virtue of the unforeseeable: "mobile and changing," "difficult to govern," the *Letter to M. d'Alembert* already said. Like "dice," they defy both "force and reason."* *De facto* and *de jure,* opinion can change *from one day to the next* [*de jour en jour*]. Literally *ephemeral,*** it has no status because it does not have to be stable, not even constantly unstable, for it sometimes "takes its time." A first ambiguity stems from this *rhythm:* if it had a proper place (but that is the whole question), public opinion would be the forum for a permanent and transparent discussion. It would be opposed to non-democratic powers, but also to its own political representation. Such repre-

*Jean-Jacques Rousseau, "The Letter to M. D'Alembert on the Theatre" in *Politics and the Arts,* trans. Allan Bloom (Ithaca: Cornell University Press, 1968), p. 74.—Trans.

**From the Greek *ephemeros,* "lasting only one day."—Trans.

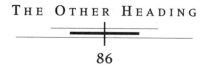
sentation will never be adequate to it, for it breathes, deliberates and decides according to other rhythms. One can also fear the tyranny of shifts in opinion. The speed, the "from day to day" [*au jour le jour*], even in the "long run," sometimes affects the rigor of the discussion, the time of the "coming to awareness," with opinion sometimes lagging paradoxically behind the representative agencies. Thus on the subject of capital punishment, we believe that we know (but especially by way of opinion polls!) that the majorities would not be the same *today* (1) in the Parliament, (2) during a referendum, (3) in "opinion polls" or sociological studies. There is no shortage of examples of such discordances or differences in rhythm. In order to gain recognition for the immigrants' right to vote in local elections, the campaign launched by SOS Racism* would have to inform and convince an opinion that would *then* be heard by the parliamentary majority;

*An organization devoted to fighting racism in France.—Trans.

but the President of the Republic, then a candidate, had *already* announced his personal "opinion" on the subject and, even better, had given his point of view on the present state of affairs, that is, on the lagging behind of public opinion and even of the Parliament—something that is not without effect on either of them. A disconcerting typology. How does one here identify public opinion? Does it take *place*? Where is it given to be seen, and *as such*? The wandering of its proper body is also the ubiquity of a specter. It is not *present as such in any of these spaces.* Exceeding electoral representation, public opinion is *de jure* neither the *general will* nor the *nation,* neither *ideology* nor the sum total of *private* opinions analyzed through sociological techniques or modern poll-taking institutions. It does not speak in the first person, it is neither subject nor object ("we," "one"); one *cites* it, one makes it speak, ventriloquizes it ("the real country" [*pays réel*], "the silent majority," Nixon's "moral majority," Bush's "mainstream," etc.), but this "average" [*moyenne*] sometimes retains the

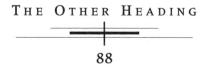
power to resist the means [*moyens*] "proper to guiding public opinion," to resist this "art of changing" public opinion that, as Rousseau again says, "neither reason, nor virtue, nor laws" have.

2. Now, this god of a negative politology can give no sign of life, in broad daylight, without a certain *medium*. The *daily* rhythm essential to it presupposes the widespread distribution of something like a *newspaper*, a *daily*. This techno-economic power allows opinion to be constituted and recognized as *public* opinion. Although these categories today appear hardly adequate, the newspaper is supposed to secure a place [*lieu*] of public visibility proper to *informing, forming, reflecting,* or *expressing,* thus to *representing,* an opinion that would there find the *milieu* of its freedom. This correlation between the *daily* or *quotidian*—be it written or audiovisual—and the history of public opinion largely exceeds what is called the "opinion press." Valuable and dangerous, more and more "refined," opinion polls adjust themselves at a rhythm that will never be that of political or labor

union representation. For they see the light of day in a press that often retains the initiative and power. Finally, we now know, and the newspaper or daily *produces* the newness of this news as much as it *reports* it, that public opinion is no longer *in our day* what it was yesterday and from the beginnings of its history.

3. For the phenomenon was never *natural,* that is to say, universal. No more in fact than everydayness as a major category of the social rhythm ever was. Before asking about the supposed "reality" of public opinion *today,* as well as about the cinematography of its silhouette, it is necessary to recall that the phantom has a *story,* a *history:* it is European, recent, and heavily scanned. The discourse on opinion is certainly as old as the world: *doxa* or "opinion" (which is not exactly the same thing) no doubt has equivalents in non-Western cultures. But as for the history of *public* opinion, it seems to be linked to the political discourse of Europe. It is a modern *artifact* (the premises of the American and French Revolutions here provide the most

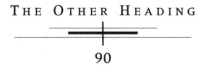
visible landmark), even if a "high point" was prepared by the tradition of a political philosophy. Under this or any other name, I do not believe that anyone has spoken seriously of public opinion without the model of parliamentary democracy and as long as an apparatus of laws (in France, from article XI of the Declaration of Human Rights* to the law of 1881 concerning the freedom of the press) did not permit or promise the formation, expression, and especially the "publication" of this opinion *outside* of these political or corporative representations.

If it is not electoral in the moment proper to it, opinion, as its name indicates, is called upon to pronounce itself by means of a *judgment*. This judgment is not some knowledge, but an engaged evaluation, a voluntary act. It always takes the form of a "judgment" (yes or no) that must exercise a power of control

---

*Article XI of the *Déclaration des droits de l'homme* states: "The unrestrained communication of thoughts and opinions being one of the most precious rights of man, every citizen may speak, write, and publish freely, provided he is responsible for the abuse of this liberty in cases determined by the law."—Trans.

and orientation *over* this parliamentary democracy. But, from the point of view of the properly political decision, this considerable potency always remains "potential." And within invisible borders. It takes place neither inside nor outside. It is situated outside statutory representation, but this outside can be recognized as the outside of an *independent public opinion* only within parliamentary democracies and representative structures: *in view of a possible vote* and an intervention *within* or *on* representation. The paradigmatic moment: the Petition of Grievances [*Cahiers de Doléances*].* As the place of a potential electorate, public opinion is an assembly of citizens called upon *to decide, by means of a judgment,* issues that are within the competence of legal representations, *but also* issues that escape them, at least provisionally, in a zone that is being extended and differenti-

---

*Traditionally, a list of demands addressed to the king or sovereign by some group or class within the state. During the French Revolution, petitions of grievances were important documents for the deputies of the Estates-General who received them from the electoral assemblies, who in turn received them from the general electorate.—Trans.

ated today in an accelerated way, thereby posing serious questions about the present functioning, if not the very principles, of liberal democracy. Just recall the demonstrations in favor of "private education," the "coordinations" of students or nurses, the debates surrounding RU 486, AIDS, drug addiction, or condoms, even the Scorsese film* (I am speaking here about speeches, declarations, or demonstrations—these elements of opinion—and not about the bombs intended to put an end to all that). But everything that is not of the order of judgment, decision, and especially representation escapes *both* present-day democratic institutions *and* public opinion as such. This couple is joined, conjugated, by the possibility of evaluation in the form of the *judgment that decides* (yes or no) and that is produced in a *representation.* Opinion surveys try to escape this law, on the one

---

*Derrida is referring to *The Last Temptation of Christ,* which was picketed throughout France and even provoked a bomb attack on a movie theatre in the Latin Quarter of Paris. RU 486 is what is known in the U.S. as the French abortion pill.—Trans.

hand, by exceeding electoral themes and immediately political decisions and, on the
other, by multiplying the evaluations in per-
centages (more or less) rather than in an alternative (yes or no). But a discourse
concerns public opinion *as such* only if it an-
ticipates a legislative debate and if the "more
or less" announces a "yes or no." What then
becomes of this reserve of experience, evaluation, and even determination (the "trends,"
"tastes," and "customs") that is not of the
order of judgment (yes or no) and representation, in any sense of this word? It is here that
one can question the authority of opinion—
not in its content but in its form of pre-elec-
toral judgment; and one can even question
the distinction private/public whose rigor
will always be threatened by language, by
language alone, and thus already with the
slightest mark. What public—and thus political—place is to be made for this kind of question?

A "government of opinion" can play with
opinion, invent it or invoke it against instituted representations. But this can be done,

or said, only in an at least formal democracy.
A popular dictatorship or a totalitarian regime is not a government of opinion (and
what is seeing the light of day today in the
U.S.S.R. is perhaps quite simply a public
opinion). The new means of "staying up to
date," of taking the pulse of opinion at a
quasi-daily rhythm, authorizes and requires a
certain power (for example that of a head of
state or even of a democratic government) to
take into account an evolution before and beyond its expression in the Parliament, in the
parties and labor unions, to discern changes
in the majority before elections and even before a referendum. It is not that opinion is
the amorphous reservoir of an untamed
spontaneity that would exceed organizations
(parties, labor unions, etc.). Neither passive
nor active, the recent "coordinations" of students or nurses were no more "manipulated"
than they were the result of an unorganized
spontaneity. Other categories are thus necessary to conduct the analysis—and political
action—beyond this basic alternative. The
same thing goes for the relationships with in-

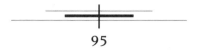
stitutions and especially with the press: public opinion does not *express itself,* if one understands by this that it exists somewhere deep down, *before* manifesting itself in broad daylight, as such, in its phenomenality. It *is* phenomenal. It is no more *produced* or *formed,* indeed *influenced* or *inflected,* than simply *reflected* or *represented* by the press. These naive or crude interpretations are rooted in a powerful philosophical discourse. Is not acting responsibly first of all to try and reconsider these interpretations? Such a task is philosophical and political, theoretical and practical; it is difficult but also dangerous, because it risks touching upon the very concept of representation, upon the "idea of representatives" that Rousseau called "modern."* But does not a democrat have the responsibility to think through the axioms or foundations of democracy? To analyze unrelentingly its historical determinations—those that, in

---

*Jean-Jacques Rousseau, *The Social Contract,* Ch. XV, trans. Charles Frankel (New York: Hafner Publishing Co., 1947), p. 85.—Trans.

1989, can be delimited and those that cannot?

For it is indeed a question of the future of democracy. The dimension of "public" space no doubt reaches its philosophical modernity with the Enlightenment, with the French and American Revolutions, or with discourses like Kant's that link the *Aufklärung*—the progress of Enlightenment and of the day—to the freedom of making *public* use of reason in all domains (even though reason is not reducible to the "opinion" that it must also submit to critique). In this post-Revolutionary modernity, the techno-economic mutation of the media marks another scansion. Following World War I, and especially in Germany, the crises that radio could provoke in the traditional space of a parliamentary democracy gave rise to heated debates. (Cf. Ferdinand Tönnies's *La critique de l'opinion publique* [*Kritik der öffentlichen Meinung*] [Berlin: J. Springer] of 1922, or the works of Carl Schmitt, whose influence is still alive, whether he is cited or not, (on the) left and (on the) right, in every analysis of public space, for example in Habermas.* These questions cannot be taken up here—let us not forget the constraints of the press, which are not only quantitative: they also impose models of readability. All the stakes that we are discussing at this very moment are concentrated in what I must entrust here to the ellipsis of a telegram. Can one speak seriously of the press in the press? Yes and no, in contraband.) These debates have not become outdated: think of the *immediately* international effects of the television of tomorrow on a public opinion that was first considered to be national. Think of the transformations that an opinion poll technique introduces when it can literally accompany and, even better, produce the televisual event ("The Hour of Truth"!).** Like the press, this technique can surely give a voice to minorities deprived of institutional representation; it can correct errors and injustices; but this "de-

---

*Cf. Derrida's "The Politics of Friendship," trans. Gabriel Motzkin, *The Journal of Philosophy,* vol. 85, no. 11, pp. 632–45.—Trans.
**A popular French TV talk show.—Trans.

mocratization" never legitimately represents. It never represents without filtering or screening—let us repeat it—a "public opinion." The "freedom of the press" is democracy's most precious good, but to the degree that one has not at least granted rights, effectively, in laws and in customs, to the questions that we have just been asking, this fundamental "freedom" remains to be invented. *Every day.* At least. And democracy along with it.

—*What system is to be invented, then, so that the formally free press does not function as censorship?*

—It is in fact in the chapter "Of Censorship" that the *Social Contract* treats this "kind of law" that the "judgment" of public opinion is. But can we here trust in the opposition *form/content* ? Is it enough to give content to a form in order to advance the freedom of the press, that is, the freedom of a right that will never go without duty or without the recognition of a freedom "before the press"? It is necessary to maintain formal rigor, for with-

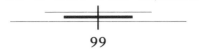
out it no right is protected; and so it is necessary to invent more refined procedures, a more differentiated legislation, one better fitted to the techno-economic mutations of the "free market." An infinite task, not only because there will always be something more or something better to be done, but because of a *principial contradiction.* A democracy must surely be vigilant so that censorship (in the legal sense: this "criticism" that has, Kant says, public "power") does not win back lost ground.* It is also necessary to fight against the effects of "censorship" in the large sense, against a "new censorship," if I may put it this way, that threatens liberal societies; to fight against accumulation, concentration, and monopoly; in short, against all quantitative phenomena that might marginalize or reduce to silence anything that cannot be measured on their scale. But one cannot, for all that, plead *simply* for plurality, dispersion,

---

*Immanuel Kant, *Religion within the Limits of Reason Alone,* trans. Theodore M. Greene and Hoyt H. Hudson (New York: Harper & Brothers, 1960), p. 7.—Trans.

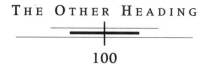
or fractioning, for the mobility of screening places or of the subjects who occupy them. For certain socio-economic forces might once again take advantage of these marginalizations and this absence of a general forum. How then to open the avenue of great debates, accessible to the majority, while yet enriching the multiplicity and quality of public discourses, of agencies of evaluation, of "scenes" or places of visibility, etc.? A wager, an aporia? This invention, at once impossible and necessary, can only be announced on the basis of another imperative: the unity or "centrality" of the democratic forum must not be confused with that of the mass, with concentration, homogeneity, or monopoly. For the "new censorship"—and this is the strength of its ruse—combines concentration *and* fractionalization, accumulation *and* privatization. It de-politicizes. This terrible logic is not restricted to the "audiovisual," though it is more perceptible there. It is at work as soon as an interpretation, that is to say, a selective evaluation, informs a "fact." No information escapes it.

This is all too evident in what is called the "cultural" press (arts, literature, philosophy, etc.) and in all those "refined," overdetermined, super-coded evaluations that do not *immediately* induce public opinion as political judgment or electoral decision. Each time a media institution controls market phenomena on a massive scale, it seizes and censures just as massively; it dogmatizes, no matter what its real eclecticism or facade of liberalism, its virtues or vices, may be, no matter whether it captivates or bores, whether one finds it distinguished or crude or both. When a single judge, no matter what one may think of his or her particular talents, is entrusted somewhere with a monopoly of evaluation, of screening, of exhibiting in full daylight, he or she determines sales in the supermarkets of culture. A work is thus relegated far from the court, into the darkness of a *quasi-private* enclosure, if it does not fulfill the conditions of visibility in this great little mirror that fascinates as it distorts, that screens and deflects toward itself so much energy, that interrupts the conversation, makes the body and the so-

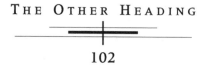
cial gaze conform to a new physiology, and then finally projects abroad the latest icons of the national culture. Today, on this scale, a book must sell and—there is a difference— be read at more than ten thousand copies in order to be something more than a confidential and *quasi*-private correspondence. The result is that what is called "difficult" research, that which resists the stereotypes of the image or of narration, which does not submit to the norms of the culture—thereby represented in its "average" (in the singular, "opinion" always means the "average")—is excluded from the scene: occulted, deprived of the *light of day. As a result, such research is judged* to be more and more "obscure," "difficult," indeed "unreadable," and so it becomes what one says it is and wants it to be: inaccessible. And the cycle accelerates. Whatever may be said of the quality of our "cultural" media, is it a coincidence that our country is, in Europe, the one in which people read the least? That our libraries are in a disastrous state, almost too shameful to admit? And that—a problem inextricably

linked to these—our schools and universities, the privileged places for the "formation of judgment," are undergoing such hardships?

But once again, let us not simplify things. Perhaps it is also necessary to take account of other rhythms and trajectories. Perhaps it is necessary not to let oneself be fascinated by quantitative immediacy. Like the schools, the press contributes to the quality of democratization. Access to the average is often a form of progress. Certain newspapers can, depending on the situation, accentuate *or* denounce, for better *or* for worse, official evaluations (those, for example, of the academic profession, of certain academic bodies). But is the power of the media unlimited? It too is evaluated from one day to the next by a public that is not always silent. This heterogeneous power can sometimes criticize itself, from one part of its large body to another. Is it not in the end judged over a longer period of time and according to criteria that remain necessarily indecipherable to it? If it contributes to mass successes that are forgotten a

month later, does not it too risk being forgotten? Untimely developments that escape its grid of readability might one day take over without any resistance at all. As for the future course of a work, the quality of ten readers, as we know, sometimes plays a more determining role than the immediate reality of ten thousand buyers. What would our great media machines do with Rimbaud or Lautréamont, with Nietzsche or Proust, with a Kafka or a Joyce of 1989? They were at first saved by a handful of readers (a minimal listening audience), but what readers! Perhaps this analogy already suffers from anachronism—alas—for the *intrinsic* history of those episodes was no doubt linked to its *outside* and, whether one denies it or not, to a structure of "public space" that is now outdated. But the limited edition still retains a chance: *quasi*-private, it nonetheless has access to public space. Between the two, *samizdat*.* Given these rhythms and qualitative

---

*Russian for self-edition. A general term for a group of means to distribute works prohibited by censorship.—Trans.

differences, the porosity of a border between "private" and "public" seems more incalculable than ever. Each event comes into contact with the law, like contraband smugglers or members of the resistance. Passage is never assured. Public opinion is not an incalculable average, but there is perhaps the incalculable in it. It is simply that the incalculable, *if there is any*, never *presents* itself; it is not, it is never, the theme of some scientific or philosophical objectification.

The only choice is thus not concentration or dispersion. The alternative would rather be between the *unilateral* and the *multilateral* in the relations of the media to the "public," to the "publics." *Responsibility*, that is, the freedom *of* the press and *before* the press, will always depend upon the effectiveness of a "right of *response*,"* a right that allows the citizen to be more than the fraction (the pri-

---

*Though *le droit de réponse* is usually known in English as the "right of reply," we have opted for the "right of response" since it maintains the relationship with responsibility. *Droit de réponse* was also the name of a controversial though popular French TV talk show.—Trans.

vate, deprived [*privée*] fraction, in sum, and more and more so) of a passive, consumer "public," necessarily cheated because of this. Is there democracy without reciprocity?

—*How does one extend the right of response to such a degree?*

—France is one of the few countries that recognize the *right of rectification* (on the part of public powers to which it is reserved) and, more generally, the *right of response*. This is a fundamental right. Yet one can only exercise it (going strictly by the law—I am not speaking about ethics or politics) in very restricted conditions. Error or falsification, omission, interpretative violence, abusive simplification, the rhetoric of insinuation, stupidity as well, all these things most often remain without any public and immediate response, on the radio, on television, or in the newspapers. And of course, massively, in books. Even when the juridical or technical difficulties do not discourage one in advance, a response is in general neutralized by the place, framework, and delays. As long as the right of response does not receive its full extension and effectiveness (again the infinite task), democracy will be accordingly limited. Only in the press? Certainly, but the press is everywhere *today:* it gives (itself), in any case, (out to be) the day itself, it brings (itself) to the light of day [*(se) donner . . . (pour) le jour*]. It brings public space to the light of day, gives the light of day to it, to its publicity. It brings to light the day itself, gives daylight to the day itself. *Thus the right of response hardly exists.* Why does one so often pretend (a fiction *of* democracy) to ignore the violence of this dissymmetry, along with what can or cannot be reduced in it? Why the hypocrisy, the denial or the blindness before the all-too-evident? Why is this "all-too-evident" at once as clear as the light of day and the most nocturnal face of democracies as they are, *presently?*

Given that good will (which is indispensable) will not be enough to change things that no longer fall under a logic of simple "consciousness" and of a juridical—that is, inadequate—concept of responsibility, given

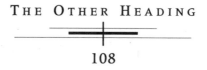
that technical procedures and formal legality (which are indispensable and can always be improved) will never reach the end of this immeasurability, given that whenever it is a question of response and responsibility, of address and destination, etc., the philosophical concepts that we have inherited have never sufficed; given all this, one will recall the French Revolution only by appealing to other revolutions. The memory of a promise, such an appeal or call seeks a new tone. It, no doubt, will no longer be "revolutionary," and it must take its time—beyond the "revolutionary *day*" [*journée révolutionnaire*].* Nothing guarantees it this, and I can say no more about it in a page.**

"Yet another effort."***

---

*During the French Revolution, "revolutionary days" were called to mark, celebrate, and renew the Revolution.—Trans.

**Derrida is referring to his agreement with the editors of *Le Monde de la Révolution française* that his article not exceed a single newspaper page.—Trans.

***The Marquis de Sade, *Philosophy in the Bedroom,* in *The Marquis de Sade,* compiled and translated by Richard Seaver and Austryn Wainhouse (New York: Grove Press, 1965), p. 296. The complete line is: "Yet another effort, / Frenchman, / If you would become republicans."—Trans.

And yet another word, if you will allow me, the very word that you gave me to begin with—*today*. Already the days are numbered: at *another speed*, the day is announced, the day is coming, when the *day* reaches its end. The day is announced when the day (the visibility of the image and the publicity of the public, but also the unity of daily rhythm, but also the phenomenality of the political, but also perhaps, and at the same time, its very essence) will no longer be the *ratio essendi*, the reason or the ration of the telemetatheoretical effects that we have just been speaking about.

Has the day ever been the measure of all things, as one pretends to believe?

In its first edition, this opinion, I hardly dare say this fiction, remains the most widely shared thing in the world.

NOTES

1. *La Crise de l'esprit, Note* (ou *L'Européen*), in *Essais quasi politiques, Oeuvres* (Paris: Gallimard, la Pléiade, 1957), t. I, p. 1004 [translated by Denise Folliot and Jackson Mathews as "The European," in *History and Politics* (New York: Bollingen, 1962), pp. 311–12]. (If I may be allowed to indicate in passing that with regard to Europe and Spirit, whether it be in Valéry or Husserl, more implicitly in Hegel and Heidegger, this conference develops, and thus presupposes to a certain extent, reflections published in other works, most noticeably in *De l'esprit: Heidegger et la question* [Paris: Galilée, 1987] [*Of Spirit. Heidegger and the Question,* trans. Geoffrey Bennington and Rachel Bowlby (Chicago: University of Chicago Press, 1989)].) The long note that this book consecrates to Valéry in particular (p. 97 [pp. 122–24]) is, in the end, only expanded upon a bit here. It began a "comparative analysis of these three discourses—Valéry's, Husserl's, and Heidegger's—on the crisis or destitution of spirit as spirit of Europe," and it had already been called for by one of Valéry's questions:

> Must such phenomena as democracy, the exploitation of the globe, and the general spread of technology, all of which presage a *deminutio capitis* for Europe . . . must these be taken as absolute decisions of fate? Or have we some freedom *against* this threatening conspiracy of things? (*La Crise de l'esprit, Deuxième Lettre,* I,

p. 1000 ["The Crisis of Spirit," "Second letter," *History and Politics*, p. 36]).

To the question, "But who, after all, is European?" [*History and Politics*, p. 316], that is, to the question of our "distinction" and that which "has most profoundly distinguished us from the rest of humanity," Valéry responds by first following the history of what he calls the "capital" or "the *City par excellence*" [*History and Politics*, p. 317], namely, Rome, after Jerusalem and Athens. He concludes these few pages by defining *Homo Europaeus* by distinctive traits other than race, language, and customs. He still defines him by spirit, but the essence of spirit manifests itself, it offers its phenomenal image to an economico-metaphysical determination (at once subjective and objective) of being as need and desire, work and will. Europe is the name of that which leads the desiring or willing subject toward his objectivizable *maximum*. Capital belongs to the series of Europe's phenomenal manifestations.

> In power and precise knowledge, Europe still, even today, greatly outweighs the rest of the world. Or rather, it is not so much Europe that excels, but the European Spirit, and America is its formidable creation. (See on this subject *"L'Amérique, projection de l'esprit européen,"* t. II, pp. 987ff. ["America: A Projection of the European Spirit," in *History and Politics*, p. 329ff.].)
>
> Wherever that Spirit prevails, there we witness the maximum of *needs*, the maximum of *labor, capital,* and *production,* the maximum of *ambition* and *power,* the maximum *transformation of external Nature,* the maximum of *relations* and *exchanges.*

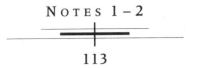
All these maxima taken together are Europe, or the image of Europe.

Moreover, the source of this development, this astonishing superiority, is obviously the quality of the individual man, the average quality of *Homo Europaeus.* It is remarkable that the European is defined not by race, or language, or customs, but by his aims and the amplitude of his will. . . . Etc. (I, p. 1014 [*History and Politics,* p. 323]).

One will have noticed that by posing in this way the question of what *distinguishes* Europe and what *calls* it from its absolute singularity, Valéry is well aware that he must treat the *name* of Europe, the name *Europe,* as an absolutely proper name. In this unique and irreplaceable reference, it is a matter of an individual whose identity is personal, perhaps more personal than all European persons; for the latter participate in this absolute spirit that makes them possible. Hence the form of the definition or description: "All these maxima taken together are *Europe* . . . "—not *l'Europe.**

2. Tome I, p. 995 [*History and Politics,* p. 31]. I will have had here to limit myself merely to proposing, in passing or in the end, a program for reading (census, logical indexing, interpretation) the uses of the *capitalistic* lexicon and its stakes in Valéry's text. Be it a question of history or of historical knowledge, of the event or of the concept, it would always be necessary to recapture the "capital moment" (II, p. 915 [*History and*

---

*By dropping the definite article, Valéry seems to be treating Europe not as a thing—a place or continent—but as a person with a proper name.—Trans.

Politics, p. 6]). The "notion of an *event,* which is funda-
mental," would not have been thought or "re-
thought" (II, p. 920 [*History and Politics,* p. 11]) by the
historian, precisely because "that capital moment
when precise and specialized definitions and conventions replace meanings that are confused and statisti-
cal in origin has not yet arrived for history" (II, p. 915
[*History and Politics,* p. 6]). In other words, what has not
yet happened to history, as science, is the capital *event*
of a concept, of a possibility of thinking that would
allow it first to think the *event* as such. Further on, it is
again the expression "capital event" that describes the
appearance of a configural and identifying *unity,* of a
coordination or *system* of correspondence in the progress and organization of sensible knowledge. Valéry
emphasizes: "Sight, touch, and act are coordinated in
a sort of multiple entry table, which is the tangible
world, and finally—a capital *event*—it turns out that a
certain system of correspondences is necessary and
sufficient for a uniform adjustment of all the visual
sensations to all the sensations of the skin and mus-
cles" (II, p. 922 [*History and Politics,* p. 13]). This event
is not only capital, it is the event of *capital* itself,
namely, of what is called the *head.*

And in addition, or as a result, beyond historical
knowledge, this discourse immediately and at the same
time touches upon the historical *thing,* upon the very
fabric of events, first of all from Europe's point of
view. What would have escaped the historians is what
would have, in short, *happened to the event, come to be an
event.* The "considerable event" that, because of its
"essential singularity," would have escaped the his-

torians as well as the event's "contemporaries," is the saturation of the habitable earth and the fact that, "under the evil spell of the written word," everything is put into relation with everything else; and so *the age of the finite world has begun.*" Politics and history can no longer speculate upon the localization or "isolation of events." There is no longer any local crisis or war. The "Decline of Europe" (II, p. 927 [*History and Politics,* p. 19]) belongs to this "age of the finite world" that Europe itself has precipitated by exporting itself, and by Europeanizing the non-Europeans, awakening, instructing, and arming—these are Valéry's words— those who aspired only to "remain as they were." This last expression at least sets the tone. What the anti-colonialism or, if you prefer, the Euro-capitalist hyper-colonialism of Valéry, the *Great-European,* seems to condemn is not so much colonialism but rather the internal rivalry that will have divided the European colonialisms and disseminated the "immense capital of knowledge" constituted by "the efforts of the best brains in Europe":

> Now, *local* European politics, dominating *general* European policy and making it absurd, has led rival Europeans to export the methods and the machines that made Europe supreme in the world. Europeans have competed for profit in awakening, instructing, and arming vast peoples who, before, were imprisoned in their traditions and asked nothing better than to remain as they were. . . . There has been nothing more stupid in all history than European rivalry in matters of politics and economics, when compared, combined, and confronted with European unity and collaboration in matters of science. While the efforts of the best brains in Europe were amassing an im-

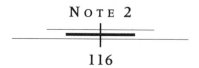
mense *capital* [my emphasis, J. D.] of usable knowl-
edge, the naive tradition of a policy based on history, a
policy of covetousness and ulterior motives, was being
pursued; and the spirit of *Little Europe,* by a kind of
treachery, handed over to the very people it meant to
dominate, the methods and instruments of power. . . .
Europe will prove not to have had the politics worthy
of her thought (II, p. 926 [*History and Politics,*
pp. 17–18]).

The equivocity of this discourse will have never
seemed so pliable, from the very best to the worst, as it
seems today (I date this today, the today of this note,
on the third day of what is called "The Gulf War"*).

---

*A thinker of fiction, convention, relay, and telecommu-
nication, Valéry was also in advance the thinker of the war
of *today,* when "the time of the finite world has begun":

> In the future, when a battle is fought anywhere in the
> world, it will be a perfectly simple matter for the
> sound of the cannon to be heard over the whole earth.
> The thunders of some future Verdun will then be *re-
> ceived* at the antipodes. It will even be possible to see
> something of the fighting, to see, at an interval of only
> three hundredths of a second, men falling six thou-
> sand miles away.

These are the opening words of a short text entitled "Hypothesis," the title for a thought that advances itself like a
hypothesis on the subject of the hypothetical character of
everything, of the Ego as the Everything, as soon as, and
from the very beginning, convention and relay establish the
regime of the simulacrum. Here are the closing words of this
"Hypothesis":

> Is not our life, insofar as it depends on what comes to
> spirit, on what seems to come from spirit and to im-
> pose itself first on spirit and then on our whole exis-
> tence—is not our life governed by an enormous,
> disorganized mass of *conventions,* most of which are
> implicit? We should be hard put to it either to express
> or to define them. Society, languages, laws, *customs,*

Especially if one considers that this was written after the fact in the "Foreword" [*Avant-propos*] to *Regards sur le monde actuel* and to the first text of this collection, "Notes on the Greatness and Decline of Europe," which, just before posing the question of "TODAY" ("What are you going to do TODAY?"), will have condemned what the politics of Europe will have done with its "capital of laws":

> Europe will be punished for her politics; she will be deprived of wines, beer, and liqueurs. And of other things. . . . Europe aspires visibly to being governed by an American Commission. Her whole policy is leading to this. Not knowing how to rid ourselves of our history, we shall be relieved of it by those happy peoples who have none, or next to none. And those happy peoples will impose their happiness on us.
>
> Europe had clearly distinguished herself from all the other parts of the world. Not by her politics but in spite of and contrary to her politics, she had developed to the utmost her freedom of spirit, had combined her passion for understanding with her will to rigorous thought, invented precise and positive speculation,

the arts, politics, in short, everything that is fiduciary in this world, every effect that is unequal to its cause, requires conventions—that is, *relays* or intermediaries, by the indirect means of which a second reality takes hold, blends with the perceptible reality of the moment, covers it over, dominates it—and is itself sometimes torn apart, disclosing the terrifying simplicity of rudimentary life. In our desires, our regrets, our quests, in our emotions and passions, and even in our effort to know ourselves, we are the puppets of nonexistent things—things that need not even exist to affect us (II, pp. 942-45 [*Aesthetics,* trans. Ralph Manheim (New York: Bollingen, 1964), pp. 229-33], Valéry's emphasis).

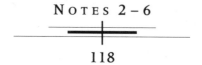
and created, by the obstinate pursuit of results that could be accurately compared and accumulated, a *capital* of powerful *laws* and procedures. Yet, her politics remained as they had always been, borrowing from the singular riches and resources I have mentioned just enough to support her primitive political practices and to furnish them with more redoubtable and barbarous weapons (II, p. 930 [*History and Politics*, pp. 227–28], my emphasis).

3. As for *fromm* and *promos*, the "pious" that also comes in the first rank, in the avant-garde of a combat, cf. Heidegger's *"Die Frage nach der Technik,"* in *Vorträge und Aufsätze*, p. 38 ["The Question Concerning Technology," trans. William Lovitt, in *Martin Heidegger: Basic Writings*, ed. David Farrell Krell (San Francisco: Harper & Row, 1976), p. 316] and the remarks that I devote to it in *De l'esprit*, p. 149 [*Of Spirit*, pp. 130ff]; concerning *Ort*, the place and the tip of the lance, cf. in particular Heidegger, *Unterwegs zur Sprache*, p. 37 [*On the Way to Language*, trans. Peter D. Hertz (New York: Harper & Row, 1971), p. 159].

4. I take the liberty of referring once again here to *De l'esprit: Heidegger et la question* [*Of Spirit: Heidegger and the Question.*]

5. It is the impossible possibility of a "logic" that I try to formulate (though it is by definition never absolutely formalizable) in *Psyché: Inventions de l'autre* (Galilée, 1987), particularly, in the first essay of that collection [*Psyche: Inventions of the Other*, trans. Catherine Porter, in *Reading de Man Reading*, ed. Wlad Godzich and Lindsay Waters (Minneapolis: University of Minnesota Press, 1989)].

6. Valéry the Mediterranean, Valéry the European,

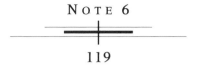
wanted to be, in just as exemplary a way, the thinker of Paris. There is nothing surprising in this, and it is this logic that we are analyzing here. In *Présence de Paris* ["Paris Is Here"], of 1937, the most noble and most serious of tasks comes down not only to "thinking PARIS" but to thinking the identity of this capital (whose name Valéry writes in capital letters twenty-six times in five pages) and its identity with "spirit itself," "the awareness of an unrelenting mission of the spirit": "I fancy that to think PARIS may be compared, or may be confounded, with *thinking spirit itself*" (*Présence de Paris*, II, p. 1012 ["Paris Is Here," in *Poems in the Rough*, trans. Hilary Corke (New York: Bollingen, 1969), pp. 266–67]. Valéry had previously formulated a project that will be accomplished only by being inverted, according to the very logic of being, that is, according to the *logos* of absolute spirit (and) of the capital. Spirit and the capital are presented or represented in each other. The inhabitant of the capital is then "thought" by the habitat earlier than he thinks. First moment: "Whence is born in me this daunting and absurd desire: to think PARIS." But, after four marvelous pages comes the ultimate moment of the coming to awareness and the reversal: "To think PARIS? . . . The more one tries, the more one feels that, on the contrary, it is by PARIS that one is thought." Just before this, the "figure" of the face [*la "figure" de la figure*] had guided the analysis of this capital of capitals. One actually *looks the capital in the face*. One distinguishes the face, the head and the forehead:

> For she is the head of France, in which are sited the country's organs of perception and most sensitive re-

actions. Her beauty and light give France a countenance on which at moments the whole intelligence of the land may be seen visibly to burn. When strong feelings seize our people, it is to this brow the blood mounts, irradiating it with a mighty flush of pride (II, p. 1015 [*Poems in the Rough,* p. 270]).

The "exemplarist" logic that we are here trying to recognize had in fact driven Valéry, ten years earlier, in the *Fonction de Paris* ["Function of Paris," in *History and Politics*] (1927), to present this capital not only as a cosmopolitical metropolis, a fate that it shares with other great *Western* cities ("Every great city in Europe or America is cosmopolitan" (II, p. 1007 [*History and Politics,* p. 397]), but as the capital of capitals. This capital "is distinguished" from all other capitals. Indeed, "distinction" will be the master word of this discourse. Paris *distinguishes itself* in two respects that are capitalized. *On the one hand,* it is the capital of the country in *every* domain, and not only, as in other countries, the political *or* economic *or* cultural capital.

> To be in itself the political, literary, scientific, financial, commercial, voluptuary, and sumptuary capital of a great country; to embody its whole history; to absorb and concentrate its whole thinking substance as well as all its credit and nearly all its monetary resources and assets, all this being both *good and bad* for the nation that this city crowns—it is in this that Paris *distinguishes itself* from all other giant cities (II, p. 1008 [*History and Politics,* pp. 398–99], my emphasis).

On the other hand, by being distinguished in this way, the *exemplary* capital, our capital, is no longer simply the capital of a country, but the "head of Europe," and thus of the world, the capital of human society in general, or even better, of "human sociability":

This Paris, whose character is the result of long experience and an endless number of historical vicissitudes; Paris that in the space of three hundred years has twice or three times been the *head* of Europe, three times conquered by the enemy, the theater of half a dozen political revolutions, the creator of an amazing number of reputations, the destroyer of countless stupidities, constantly summoning to herself both *the flower and the dregs of the race,* has made herself the *metropolis of various liberties and the capital of human sociability* (II, p. 1009 [*History and Politics,* p. 400], my emphasis).

We must neglect neither the insistent ambiguity of this evaluation nor the abyssal potentialities of this equivocation. In 1927, the "Function of Paris" spoke of everything in the capital that was at once "good and bad for the nation that this city crowns," [p. 399], thus for the head, and it associated "the immense advantages" with "the grave dangers of such a concentration": with "the flower" are associated, like a fatal parasite, "the dregs of the race" [*History and Politics,* p. 400]. What distinguishes, what distinguishes *itself,* is always the most threatened, the best being always right up against the worst. Privilege is by definition a delicateness in danger. The danger comes from abroad, from the foreigner, not only from the European foreigner but from a foreigner who comes from even further away to contaminate, who comes, more precisely, from other shores, from an outside of Europe—and who threatens spirit itself, the "spirit of Paris" inasmuch as it incarnates spirit itself. Shortly after having spoken about the "dregs of the race," Valéry in fact concludes:

The mounting credulity in the world, due to boredom with entertaining clear ideas and *the rise of exotic peoples*

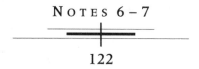
to civilized life, threatens what used to distinguish the spirit of Paris. We have known it as the capital of quality and the capital of criticism. We have every reason to fear for these glories, wrought by centuries of delicate experiment, enlightenment, and choice [*History and Politics,* p. 400, my emphasis].

Ten years later, on the eve of the war, Valéry recalls the negative effects of capital "concentration"; he associates with it, more or less deliberately, the value of "jealousy," and—this is in 1937—uses the expression "concentration camp," a camp that "consumes" "every Frenchman who *distinguishes* himself." I emphasize:

Yet PARIS clearly *distinguishes* herself from her fellow million-headed monsters, the NEW YORKS, LONDONS, PEKINGS . . . our BABYLONS. . . . For in none of them has every kind of élite of a nation been so *jealously concentrated,* for so many centuries, so that by her judgment alone each value takes its place in the scale of values, submitting to her comparisons, facing her criticism, *jealousy.* . . . This invaluable traffic could scarcely subsist except where, for centuries, every kind of élite of a great nation has been *jealously* called together and fenced in. To this *concentration camp* is destined every Frenchman who *distinguishes himself.* PARIS beckons him, draws him, demands him, and, sometimes, *consumes* him. (II, pp. 1014–15 [*Poems in the Rough,* pp. 269–70]).

7. "*La liberté de l'esprit,*" II, p. 1093 ["The Freedom of Spirit," in *History and Politics,* p. 186]. A few pages later, Valéry makes in passing a somewhat elliptical remark that seems to me to be of great importance, as long as one follows its implications, perhaps even be-

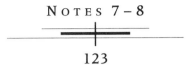
yond what Valéry intended by it. Valéry in effect determines *freedom* as *response:* " . . . the idea of freedom is not *instinctive* [*première*] in us; it never comes unless it is called. I mean it is always *a response*" (II, p. 1095 [*History and Politics* , p. 207]).

8. The logic of this text is also an *analogic*. In truth, it stems entirely from a dissymmetrical analogy between spirit and value. Spirit is a value among others, certainly, like gold, wheat, or oil, but it is also the source of all value, thus the exceeding value, the absolute and therefore sublime surplus value of the priceless. Spirit is one of the categories of the analogy *and* the incomparable condition, the transcendental, the transcategorial of the whole economy. It is an example and an exemplary example, the example *par excellence.* There is no other. Since Valéry says this so well in another way, I am content with gathering together a few quotations around what he himself calls, as if in passing, "the capital point":

> It is a sign of the times . . . that today it is not only necessary but imperative to interest people's spirits in the fate of Spirit—that is, in their own fate. . . . They had faith in spirit, but what spirit? . . . what did they mean by this word? . . . The word is indecipherable, since it refers to the source and value of all other words [*History and Politics,* p. 186].

Present, immanent in all that it is not, in all the values that are not as valuable as it is, this word can, from now on and without any risk, enter into analogy, into the parallelism of economy and the economy of parallelism, between capital and capital. It is "the very thing," the "capital point," the thing itself that is di-

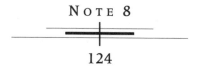
vided between the two registers or two regimes of the analogy. For example:

> I spoke, I believe, of the decline and collapse, before our very eyes, of the values of our life; and with the word *value* I brought together under one term, one sign, values of the material and the spiritual order.
>
> *Value* is the very thing I wish to talk about, the capital point to which I should like to draw your attention.
>
> We are today witnessing a true and gigantic transmutation of values (to use Nietzsche's excellent phrase), and in giving to this lecture the title "Freedom of Spirit" I am simply alluding to one of those essential values that nowadays seem to be suffering the same fate as material values.
>
> So, in saying *value,* I mean that *spirit* is a value, just as *oil, wheat,* and *gold* are values.
>
> I said *value* because an appraisal, an assessment of importance is involved, and also because there is a price to be discussed—the price we are willing to pay for the value we call *spirit.*
>
> . . . On that market, *spirit* is "weak"—it is nearly always falling. . . . You see that I am borrowing the language of the stock exchange. . . . I have often been struck by the analogies that arise, in the most natural way in the world, between the life of spirit in all its manifestations and the various aspects of economic life. . . . In both enterprises, in the economic as in the spiritual life, you will find the same basic notions of *production* and *consumption.* . . .
>
> Moreover, in either case we may equally well speak of capital and labor. *Civilization is a kind of capital* that may go on accumulating for centuries, as certain other kinds of capital do, and absorbing its compound interest (II, pp. 1077–82 [*History and Politics,* pp. 189–91]).

Valéry emphasizes all this; and he claims not to be proposing here a "mere comparison, more or less po-

etic," not to be moving, through "mere rhetorical arti-
fices," from material economy to spiritual economy.
To make this claim, he must confirm the at once origi-
nary and transcategorial character of the concept of
spirit, which while making the analogy possible, does
not completely belong to it. No more than *logos,* in
sum, is simply included in the analogy in which it
nonetheless participates. And in fact, beyond mere
rhetoric, spirit is *logos,* speech, or word—as Valéry literally explains. This original spiritualism indeed presents itself as a logocentrism. More rigorously still, as a
logocentrism whose birthplace is in the Mediterranean basin. Once again, it is best to quote. Valéry has
just been claiming not to have moved, through an arti-
fice of rhetoric, from material economy to spiritual
economy, and he emphasizes:

> In fact, if we look closely at the matter, we find that
> the opposite is true. *Spirit came first,* and it could not
> have been otherwise. It is the commerce of spirits that
> was necessarily the first commerce in the world, the
> very first, the one that started it all, necessarily the
> original: for before swapping goods, it was necessary
> to swap signs, and consequently a set of signs had to
> be agreed on. There is no market, no exchange with-
> out language; the first instrument of all trade is lan-
> guage. We may here repeat (giving it a suitably altered
> meaning) the famous saying: *"In the beginning was the
> Word."* It was essential that the Word should precede
> the *act* of trading. But the Word is no less than one of
> the most accurate names for what I have called *spirit.*
> Spirit and the Word in many of their uses are almost
> synonymous. The term that in the Vulgate means *word*
> is translated from the Greek *"logos ,"* which means at
> once *calculation, reason, speech, discourse, and knowledge,*
> as well as expression. Consequently, in saying that the

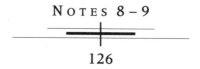
word is identical with spirit, I think I am not uttering a heresy, even in linguistics (II, p. 1084 [*History and Politics,* p. 194]).

Nothing surprising then in the fact that the "logical" and the historical are from here on homologous and indissociable: "Not only is it logically necessary that this should be so, but it can also be demonstrated historically." Those "regions of the globe" that have favored commerce are also "those regions where the production of intellectual values . . . started earliest and has been most prolific and various," those where "*freedom of spirit* has been most widely granted." And the word "market" comes back regularly (at least three times in two pages, Tome I, pp. 1005–1006 [*History and Politics,* pp. 313–14]) when it is a question of defining Europe, "this Europe of ours, which began as a Mediterranean market," Europe, "this privileged place," "the European spirit," "author of these wonders" [*History and Politics,* p. 312]. The best example, the only one in truth, the most irreplaceable, is that of the Mediterranean basin: the "example" that it "offered" is in fact unique, exemplary, and incomparable. It is therefore not an example among others, and this is why *logos* and history are no longer separated, since this example will have been "the most striking and conclusive" (II, pp. 1084–85 [*History and Politics,* p. 195]).

9. Tome II, p. 1058 [*History and Politics,* p. 436]. This should come as no surprise. It is precisely in this context that Valéry, on the subject of philosophy, links together with force two propositions that are often disjoined: the *national trait* and the *formal trait* are irreduc-

ible and indissociable in philosophy, in the discourse as well as the language of philosophy. The argumentation of these few pages is extremely intricate; it would deserve more than a note. It is still a question of "envisaging France, the role or function of France in building up the *capital* of the human spirit" (II, pp. 1047–48 [*History and Politics,* p. 426], my emphasis). Very schematically, let us say that if, on the one hand, Valéry gives the form of a concession and a *hypothesis*—"it is not impossible that," "this is quite possible"—to the proposition concerning the *national trait* that would mark all philosophy, it is precisely in looking in an exemplary way toward French philosophy that he emphasizes the *formal trait* and vigorously advances a *thesis* concerning it. One could call this thesis formalist were it not for the fear of making things more inflexible by providing an easy argument to all those who confuse attention to form, language, writing, rhetoric, or the "text" with a subjective formalism and a renunciation of the concept. One must be able to take into account the national trait and the formal trait without nationalism or formalism—and even *in order to* elaborate a strategy of refined resistance toward them. As interesting as it may be, the Valéryian strategy seems to me incapable of avoiding these two pitfalls. The national *hypothesis* inevitably precipitates itself in a *thesis* of nationalist subjectivism. The formalist thesis is there only to serve this precipitation.

First moment, the hypothesis:

> Abstract or "pure" thought, like scientific thought, endeavors to obliterate what comes to the thinker from his race or his nation, its aim being to create values

independent of place and person. It is doubtless not
impossible to discern, or think we discern, in a system
of metaphysics or morals, the part that properly belongs to one race or nation: sometimes, indeed, nothing seems to define a certain race or nation better than
the philosophy it has produced. It is claimed that certain ideas, though expressed in all universality, are almost unthinkable outside the climate of their origin.
In a foreign land they wither away like uprooted
plants, or else they look preposterous. This may well
be (II, p. 1055 [*History and Politics,* pp. 431–32]).

Second moment, the thesis. Before recalling, and em-
phasizing, that the thesis presents itself as a "feeling"
and opens with a parenthetical "apology," let us remember the date of these pages: 1939. On this eve of
combat, when nationalist and racist eloquence in
sweeping through Europe more violently than ever,
Valéry tones down into a hypothesis his propositions
on philosophy, race, and the nation. He also apolo-
gizes when, in order to speak of his "feeling" and of
philosophy as a "question of form," he essentially
links this form to the national language and, in a singular and exemplary way, to the French language:

> It is my feeling (and I apologize for this) that philoso-
> phy is a matter of form. It is not in the least a science,
> and it should free itself from any unconditional link
> with science. To be *ancilla scientiae* is no better for phi-
> losophy than to be *ancilla theologiae.* . . . I do not say
> that I am right, which in any case would be meaning-
> less. I say . . . that anyone who speaks this language,
> to others and to himself, can neither go beyond its
> means nor escape the suggestions and associations
> that the said language has insidiously implanted in
> him. If I am French, there at the very point of my

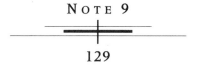
thought where thought takes shape and talks to itself, it takes shape in French, according to the possibilities and within the framework of French (ibid. [*History and Politics,* p. 432]).

What follows is an analysis, an interpretation, and an evaluation of these said possibilities; I will not engage myself in them here. Concerning philosophy more strictly, I will cite only the conclusion—for what it can allow us to think today, both with and against its author:

In France, that is the price of success for any philosophy. I do not mean that systems of ideas not conforming to this principle cannot be produced here. What I mean is that they are never truly and, as it were, *organically* assimilated. Incidentally, I find analogous French reactions in politics and the arts (II, p. 1056 [*History and Politics,* p. 434], my emphasis).

EDITOR: JACK FORD

BOOK AND JACKET DESIGNER: SHARON L. SKLAR

MANAGING EDITOR: TERRY L. CAGLE

PRODUCTION COORDINATOR: HARRIET CURRY

TYPEFACE: MERIDIEN

COMPOSITOR: SHEPARD POORMAN

PRINTER: HADDON CRAFTSMEN, INC.